D1552051

Advance Praise for *A Call to Creativity*

"The ancient practice of alchemy sought to transform common metal into precious elements. The spirit of alchemy lives in Luke Reynolds' project. He provides a purposeful framework to help teachers transform the fundamental elements of contemporary practice (standards, rubrics, aligned curricula, data-driven methods) into classroom experiences that awaken students' creativity, passion, and energy. Reynolds provides a structure for us to teach in ways where rigor and achievement unfold as opportunities for intense thought and imaginative encounters with text and writing."

—**Sam Intrator**, Professor of Education
and the Program in Urban Studies, Smith College

"Here is a book to enliven and humanize teaching and learning, benefiting teachers and students alike. But it is not for the faint of heart. A 'call to creativity' in education is also a call to risk-taking, especially in an era when many teachers feel compelled to color within the lines. As an experienced teacher, Luke Reynolds is well aware of the risks, so his book is filled with examples of exercises and lesson plans that, as he says, marry 'standards and creativity.' One look at the first exercise in the book, 'The Boston Photograph,' will convince you that this book puts wheels on high ideals in a way that can move us toward the kind of education our students deserve and our best teachers desire."

—**Parker J. Palmer**, author of *Healing the Heart of Democracy*,
The Courage to Teach, and *Let Your Life Speak*

"This marvelous new book by Luke Reynolds shows how passionate teaching is lit by soul and vulnerability, knowledge of self on the part of the teacher and a willingness to explore what can really happen in a classroom if you challenge students to engage their muscular and creative minds. Rejecting easy dualisms—that curriculum standards are bad and our current accountability environments have no place in good teaching—Reynolds presents some powerful, real examples of sample lessons that challenge students and teachers at very deep levels, and consequently, how real questions about teaching and learning are twisty, wonderful, and lifelong."

—**Kirsten Olson**, Institute for Democratic Education in America (IDEA)
and author of *Wounded by School*

"I have long thought that creativity and imagination are at the center of true learning, and that these vital human resources are roundly ignored by policymakers and even instructional discussions. Enter Luke Reynolds with his rousing justification of teaching with and for creativity and imagination, and his inspired stance and practices for doing so. His is a fresh and highly energetic and—dare I say it—creative and imaginative voice. I can't think of a more important topic or a more inspired treatment of it than this. I'm not just recommending this book, I can't wait to teach it and use it myself. Bravo, Luke Reynolds! Viva, Creativity!"

—**Jeffrey D. Wilhelm**, Professor of English Education,
Director, Boise State Writing Project

"Every chapter in *A Call to Creativity* is a real gem! Using humor and his gift as a storyteller, Luke Reynolds shows teachers not only how creativity can be woven through standards-based curricula, but why it is essential to do so if we truly want to engage our students. This book is hard to put down, and its wisdom will stay with you."

—**Christine Sleeter**, Professor Emerita, California State University,
Monterey Bay; President, National Association for Multicultural Education

(continued)

A Call to Creativity

*Writing, Reading, and Inspiring Students
in an Age of Standardization*

Luke Reynolds

Foreword by Jim Burke

Teachers College
Columbia University
New York and London

KH

Published by Teachers College Press, 1234 Amsterdam Avenue, New York, NY 10027

Library of Congress Cataloging-in-Publication Data

Reynolds, Luke, 1980–
   A call to creativity : writing, reading, and inspiring students in an age of standardization / Luke
     Reynolds ; foreword by Jim Burke.
      p. cm. — (Language and literacy series)
   ISBN 978-0-8077-5305-7 (pbk. : alk. paper) — ISBN 978-0-8077-5306-4 (hardcover : alk. paper)
   1. Creative ability—Study and teaching. 2. Language arts. 3. Motivation in education. I. Title.
   LB1590.5.R49 2012
   370.15′7—dc23   2011046312

ISBN 978-0-8077-5305-7 (paper)
ISBN 978-0-8077-5306-4 (hardcover)

Printed on acid-free paper
Manufactured in the United States of America

19 18 17 16 15 14 13 12   8 7 6 5 4 3 2 1

7/18/12

Contents

Foreword

OUR COUNTRY'S GREATEST natural (and national) resource is not in the ground, in the air, in the water, or in any other domain traditionally associated with nature. Where, then, is it to be found? Which natural resource is most vital to our country's success and survival, as well as our esteem and sense of well-being? Creativity. Our country is at its best, *we* are at our best, when we are engaged in the hard work of the mind, body, and soul during creation. Creativity is an engine, as are the heart and the head. While we have been busy creating industries, products, and processes, we have also created a culture and a country that people around the world have envied for the last 2 centuries.

That culture is not dead, nor is it dying. It is, however, in trouble. More than anything, one can't help but notice the extent to which schools are increasingly governed by fear, and fear, as someone once said to me, is a terrible counselor. It keeps us hunkered down, holding our collective breath. As more and more schools enter into Program Improvement (as my school has), more of them are governed by numbers, not names, by scores not students. I was recently invited to a district where the well-intentioned superintendent spoke with great enthusiasm (or was it relief?) about being "an 800 district." He was referring to the fact that all schools in the district had passed the 800 mark on their Annual Yearly Progress goals. Yet I never heard him, in the few minutes he spoke, say anything about students or learning.

Whenever I hear leaders—especially politicians, businesspeople, and administrators—speak in such terms, I want to ask them where their own children go to school and whether they would want them in classes designed to increase scores instead of grow minds. My own assistant superintendent sends his children to private schools; he sounds more excited talking about what they create, what they do, and what they experience in that school than I've ever heard him when talking about our own district or my school, where he used to be the principal.

So when I read Luke Reynolds's book *A Call to Creativity*, my first thought was that this was a class I wish my own children could be in, and that he was a teacher with whom they could study the deep curriculum he discusses with such passion and practical intelligence. I once heard Alfie Kohn speak, and during that talk, he discussed the idea of the 10-year test, which he explained by simply asking: What, of all you teach on any given day, will kids remember in 10 years? It's a pretty daunting standard, but that's what standards *are*: markers placed higher on the hill to show where you want to go, what you are striving to achieve.

What strikes me—and challenges and moves me as both a teacher and a parent—is the way Luke challenges himself to always exceed whatever standards he might be subject to. You get this sense of his own ambition (on his students' behalf) when you read early on about his requirement that all his students write a 50-page novella, an assignment that every student goes on to complete, many of them continuing to work on it long after they graduate. Such high expectations fill the pages of this book, and Luke talks in precise detail about how he helps his students meet and even exceed these goals.

I nodded my head all the way through this book, finding in his descriptions echoes of my own experience as a classroom teacher. It is each other that we turn to and trust the most to help us find our way. Years ago, one of the big photocopy companies learned that its repair staff were routinely getting together for lunches that often lasted as long as 2 hours. Edicts were sent out, warnings issued, threats delivered—all of which amounted to the same thing: Do not waste time on the job. Yet almost immediately, complaints came pouring in from customers. It turns out that what the repair specialists were doing over those long lunches was solving problems they had encountered that morning. They were being *creative*. They were sitting around a table, battling and trying to comprehend the *complexity* of their work. I felt, as I read Luke's book, that I was sitting at such a table over a long meal listening to and learning from a fellow craftsman who knows and understands the complexity of our work—for our work *is* complex—and embraces it, still chooses it *because* of the very demands such complexity makes on his own intelligence and ours.

This book sounds a hopeful note in the current era of teaching in general and teaching English in particular. It shows us we can still be passionate and practical, creative and collaborative at a time when too many feel it is impossible. I often think about the verbs that sum up what happens in a classroom, seeing in these words some sort of instructional DNA that might provide a reasonable window into the world of those students and their teacher. The verbs are ones that I would hope to see enacted in a rich, inquiry-based, intellectually demanding, and soulful English class: *challenge, investigate, inquire, discuss, consider*, and, of course, *create*. Luke is issuing a "call to create" to all of us, to his students, and, foremost, to himself. This call returns us—or at least invites us to return—to our roots as teachers in a profession once described in reverent terms as a vocation, which derives from the Latin word *vocare*—"to call." I accepted Luke's invitation to read this book and to write this foreword because our conversations over the last few years have been, at their core, about the sense of vocation we share as teachers, writers, and human beings. I am grateful to him for those conversations and for this book, which I encourage you to read so that you can join and contribute to this vital dialogue.

—Jim Burke, Author of *The English Teacher's Companion*

Acknowledgments

W. H. AUDEN once wrote these powerful poetic lines: "Although I love you, you will have to leap. Our dream of safety has to disappear." This call to action personifies the life of a teacher—that something deeper and bigger and wider must take the place of traditional notions of safety. And so it is crucial that I thank the people in my life that started me on the journey away from such safety and toward something riskier and more authentic.

To Robert Looney, John Robinson, and Mike Dunn: three teachers who showed me the path of fire in the English classroom.

To Harry, Kathy, Christopher, Michael, Bryan, and Matthew: a family that provides constant reminders of humor, grace, and loyalty.

To the passionate and powerful teacher-writers from whom I have gained inspiration, the belief that I am not insane, and the ability to gather my mistakes up in a heap and toss them out the window as I try again: Parker Palmer, Jim Burke, Peter Elbow, Sonia Nieto, bell hooks, Rafe Esquith, Gareth Kezier, Alan Sitomer, and Jackson Katz.

To Marilyn Cochran-Smith and Dennis Shirley, for your kind encouragement of my interests and for helpfully directing my research at the Lynch School of Education.

To Meg Lemke, an editor who sees the promise within the words, though they always need work. Your belief and excitement to make words become deeds is inspiring. To Susan Liddicoat, who carried the book from stage to stage with precision and heart. To Danny Miller, a developmental editor with enthusiasm, knowledge, and passion. And to John Bylander, a production editor whose zeal for timeliness, precision, and passion is gratifying.

To Tyler: the kind of delightful joy you reveal cracks my own heart open and bids me live with renewed vigor and hopefulness every day.

And to Jennifer: I once quoted lines from Yeats for you. But I see now that it has always been you who has loved the "pilgrim soul" in me. For this unconditional love, my mind stands incapable of rendering the depth of gratitude that my heart knows. With all that I am, *thank you, my love.*

A Call to Creativity

Introduction:
Seeing the Possible

AT FIRST, THEY don't get it.

Jacob, one of my 11th-graders who has a keen intellect, raises his hand.

"Yes, Jacob?"

He looks worried, confused. In the 4 months that Jacob has been in my American literature honors class for junior-level students, he has made his three goals very clear: (1) to attend an Ivy League college; (2) to attend an Ivy League college; (3) to attend an Ivy League college.

"But, Mr. Reynolds, this doesn't really make any sense. I mean, shouldn't we be doing what the other classes are doing?" Jacob shifts in his seat, growing more uncomfortable as he asks the question and sees my smile.

I walk toward Jacob and say, "With this project, you'll be *ahead* of the other classes. Your writing will become stronger, your understanding of text sharper, and your confidence greater. I promise."

Sarah raises her hand. I walk away from Jacob, who still looks worried, and call out, "Sarah, what's on your mind?"

She smiles slightly, then says, "But, Mr. Reynolds, you don't really think we're going to be able to write that much, do you? I mean, seriously, *50 pages*?! My sister's a sophomore in college at Brandeis, and she's never had to write anything even *close* to that much." Sarah's voice trails off as she leans back in her seat and looks down at her feet.

I take a seat on the edge of my desk. I knew it was going to be like this. In the weeks before introducing our novella assignment, I had imagined the scene numerous times in my mind. Part of me relished the chance to challenge my 11th-grade honors students with something unlike any writing assignment they had ever been given before. Another part of me asked the obvious questions: *Mutiny? Will they revolt against me? Tell my department chair I've gone insane? Report me to their parents, the principal, and the school board and have me fired?*

After all, thus far in the year, my students and I had gotten along splendidly. I had received good observation reports from my department chair and principal; my students' scores on state standardized tests had been strong and seen improvements after their time with me.

So why screw it all up?

Why introduce an assignment where my 11th-graders would have to craft 50 pages of their own original, creative fiction? Why dedicate 2 months to such an activity when this year's standardized tests were fast approaching, college applications were flying around the school like lottery tickets, and there were, indeed, high stakes?

The short answer is: I had a hunch.

It wasn't based on research (not yet, anyway—that would come later) and it wasn't based on trial tests with actual students. It was based, instead, on my own experience growing up in the public schools, teaching in the public schools, and on those conversations I had had with other English teachers where we would all lament the same thing: *Wouldn't it be great if we could get more creativity into our curriculums?*

This year, I figured, why not give it a go? What's the worst that could happen?

My hunch was that, with a large creative project that challenged students to craft something entirely original and completely of their own design, they would learn effective writing strategies and hone their skills far better than they would in the more traditional, widely marketed test-preparation curriculums. So, as I sat day after day in a tiny café near the apartment I rented, I came up with the idea of the novella assignment. (The actual assignment, along with further explanation, is included in Appendix K, as are all assignments I mention. These assignments are also online as dowloads at http://calltocreativity.blogspot.com and at http://www.tcpress.com.)

Lest I keep you in suspense, I'll be up front with the results: After 2 months, every one of my 45 eleventh-grade students had written the required 50 pages of creative fiction. I saw dramatic increases in their writing abilities. Their test scores that spring showed strong gains, and their attitudes toward writing had improved dramatically. It became common for me to overhear students talking in the hallways about what would happen next in their novellas, and it was also common to come to class on a day when their next two pages were due, only to find that many students had instead written six, seven, or eight.

Indeed, to this day—years later—I still maintain e-mail correspondence with students from those classes, and a handful are still crafting their own fiction. One still even tinkers with the novella he created in our class and has turned it into a full-length novel. And such (seemingly crazy) assignments have worked not only with these groups of 11th-grade honors students but also with alternative school students, kids in juvenile detention, middle schoolers, and college freshmen and sophomores.

I don't report this to claim a Pollyanna story of students who hated writing and then grew to love it. No; this is a much more humble tale of trial and failure. Along the way, I have made (and still make!) quite a few gaffes myself, and I continue to learn by doing, by trying to invigorate my English classrooms with creative activities, methods, beliefs, and pursuits. But I believe that there is something to offer in the notion that we can be both wildly creative and highly rigorous in our classrooms when it comes to writing, reading, and growing with students. The two are not mutually exclusive; instead, they even strengthen each other when practiced together.

I share this story as a sort of microcosm of what education in middle and secondary English classrooms might be like—what creative avenues are possible while still maintaining fidelity to the ever-increasing strictures of standardization and high-stakes testing. The novella assignment, for me, was only the start of a variety of creative assignments and activities I would eventually integrate into my curriculum.

It is still possible to incorporate highly creative activities and assignments into your English classroom in ways that can grow, challenge, awaken, and inspire your students and yourself. And it is possible—*very possible*—to do this while also adhering to those seemingly straitjacket-loving standards you've been trying to memorize and prove to your department chair or principal that you can follow.

The book you now hold in your hands is one English teacher's journey. As someone who has taught English at the middle, secondary, and college levels, I have come to believe in a simple prospect for all my students: that creativity awakens ability and enhances all that students learn, enabling them to remember information better and grow their own confidence, knowledge, and skills.

But even though this is my journey, it is also yours. As an English teacher, chances are good that you didn't pursue your dream of becoming an educator in this field in order to focus on the ever-increasing number of bound booklets that house the words "Standards for Grades 7–12, 951st Edition." Instead, it's likely that you are a creative person and that you want to see your students wake up to the potential of writing and reading by creative means.

In short, then, *A Call to Creativity* is a practical guide based on my own journey as an English teacher at three levels. Included are a variety of hands-on lessons you can use immediately. Also included are detailed explanations of longer creative projects I have used with highly successful results. In addition, I provide a brief overview of the debate over curriculum, using it to frame my argument for creativity in the classroom; I also discuss various studies of creative writing and empowerment. However, the focus of this volume is not simply on proving that creativity is effective in the English classroom. Instead, my goal is even bigger: to show how we as teachers can still be highly creative within rooms becoming more and more filled with talk of standards.

Indeed, creativity in our lives as teachers and in the lives of our students is one of our most vital needs in the 21st century. May this humble volume lend you the motivation, belief, scaffolding, and practical tools you need to be wildly creative, highly rigorous, and boldly authentic in your approach to teaching the art of two of our most sacred human endeavors: writing and reading.

CHAPTER 1

Creativity Crawls
Through the Cracks

You're an English teacher. Or you're planning to become one. Words get inside of you and shake your mind, soul, and heart. Your brain lodges visions of students wide-eyed with glee as they encounter the passages that have so deeply inspired you. Yet there is disconnect between the movie playing in your mind and the reality of where your feet take you each morning as you begin your day as a teacher. If you're anything like me, perhaps the following (somewhat) accurately portrays a snippet of your life.

YOUR (HYPOTHETICAL?) LIFE AS A DATA-DRIVEN ENGLISH TEACHER

It's 9 o'clock at night. You've just finished dinner—frozen lasagna that you thawed in the oven and ate half-cold because you were so hungry. Dishes are still in the sink. Kids (if you have them) are in bed, and you're finally sitting down for a few moments.

One moment, really.

Because now you're thinking about the next day. *What am I going to do tomorrow?* You promised yourself that you wouldn't wait this long to plan your English classes. You promised yourself that you were going to spend some serious time reviewing the new edition of the state standards your department chair discussed at the meeting last week and then come up with something creative that still toes the line. But every time you picked up the newly bound book with that word—*Standards*—on the cover, you just couldn't do it. You couldn't dive into it, feeling that if you did, you'd lose that last bit of creative energy that inspired you to become an English teacher in the first place.

"Tomorrow," you think, "what am I going to do tomorrow?" You know what your colleagues who teach the same classes are doing. There's a worksheet that addresses three of the five core standards for students' writing ability. You know the worksheet well. You helped create it. It's not very interesting. The photocopies are made, in fact, and sitting on your desk, but here it is 9 o'clock and you're up walking around again, dreading tomorrow's class. "There's got to be a better way," you're thinking, "there's got to be something more." But when your mind starts getting into other possibilities, you figure there just isn't enough time in the school day. How can you plan creative, interactive lessons, activities, and assignments that hit the standards but also get you *and* your students excited?

The truth is, you're dreading the standardized lessons and assignments just as much as your students are. You feel like hearing the word *rubric* one more time is going to make you want to shove watermelon chunks up your nose and put pretzel sticks in your ears.

If one single soul says the phrase *standardized tests* again, you feel you might lose control of your bodily functions and deck the person, even if it's the principal, the best man from your wedding, or your mom.

So, it's 9 o'clock at night; you put your head in your hands and think, "What's the point of it anymore? Spend 4 months prepping my students to do well on the state tests, and then become as drained of my passion for writing and reading as my students seem to be?"

You stop walking in circles, open the freezer, and a slight smile crosses your face. There are still two containers of Ben and Jerry's sitting there, calling out to you like love itself. One is Chunky Monkey and the other is Cherry Garcia. You choose Chunky Monkey, grab a spoon, and sigh that deep kind of sigh that can only mean one thing.

One single thing.

You're going to do the standardized, test-prep-writing-sheet thing tomorrow.

SOMETHING MORE

But wait! There's more. There's something better. There's something bigger. I promise. With the ever-increasing focus on standards, core skills, data-driven methods, and preparation for the business of high-stakes testing, there are still cracks. And it's through these cracks that a middle or secondary English teacher like yourself can find that creativity. It gets in there like mud. Or like pudding. Or like that stubborn substance that just won't ever leave a tiny crack no matter how hard you scrub and scrub.

The good news is this: *you* are that stubborn substance. You know that you became an English teacher because you wanted to do wildly creative things with your students (and with your life, for that matter). You wanted to wake your students up to the sheer power of words: the way those tiny letters can cause people to break down and cry; the way that a piece of fiction can change the course of human history; the way that creating something entirely your own—that never existed before you came along—feels like a divine miracle.

But now that you're facing a hoard of flowcharts and ever-expanding bullet lists that explain the newest standards, requirements, and high-stakes testing that you'll have to prepare your students for, you wonder: Where is the space for creativity? Rest assured: There is still room—plenty of room—for those wildly creative moments in your English classroom. *And* you can address the standards. *And* your students will be prepared for the test.

In their intrepid book *The Mindful Teacher*, Dennis Shirley and Liz MacDonald (2009) describe the process of intense standardization and accountability in our schools as a crisis for both teachers and students. However, they claim that "in spite of the push for standards, accountability, alignment, and DDDM [data-driven decision making], an alternate reality has emerged full of contradictions, messiness, and 'human, all-too-human' problems. Yet with this acknowledgment comes splendid opportunities to advance real learning—not just test-prep, or 'gaming the system'" (p. 9). If you're anything like me—anywhere near as weird as I am—then the idea of an *alternate reality* sounds pretty darn cool. A bit like watching an episode of *The Twilight Zone* with all the lights in the room turned off and eating caramel popcorn that is heavily salted while drinking orange juice through a straw that you saved for just such a moment as this.

But an alternate reality is exactly where creativity lives. Shirley and MacDonald aren't crazy (at least, I am pretty sure they aren't). They've put their fingers on the pulse of the problem and they understand that one way out of a whitewashed room is to splash some color around—in a word, to make it messy. What most of us teachers fear is that by using creative lessons and methods in our classroom when the push for standards is on, we will lose sight of requirements, hurt our students by not teaching them the skills that they need for the standardized test, or ultimately get fired. But the dualism of *either–or* thinking is dangerous here. Standards *and* creativity can coexist. Indeed, they can even thrive together. Hearing that theme song from *The Twilight Zone* yet?

REJECTING DUALISMS

In today's either–or culture, many of us have become uncomfortable with the notion of the word *and*. How can this person *and* that person be right when it comes to politics? How can we understand and value *this* idea if we've chosen to understand and value *that* one? As a deeply ingrained way of thinking, what this notion of either–or does is to render us robotic in our decisions and perceptions, unable to explore the nuances of complexity when it comes to values, decision making, and (*yes!*) education.

Another key idea from *The Mindful Teacher* is the notion that this system of dualisms must be dismantled if we want to grow as teachers and inspire our students. Instead of assuming that there is one right path that educators and researchers must follow, the notion that many tools and methods can be utilized in the pursuit of one goal emerges as a strong and viable principle. Or, as Shirley and MacDonald put it, "When there is a relentless push for practical solutions, it can be a great relief to understand that in point of fact, there often are *only* imperfect pathways forward out of complex dilemmas" (pp. 56–57). The reason standards are so appealing to policymakers and administrators is that they are perfect; they are clear, practical, and tangible guidelines around which we can all stand huddled as a crowd and say, *Look! There! Yup, that's it. That's what it's all about!* By recognizing the necessity of standards while at the same time saying that those standards need to be able to birth imperfect, sometimes messy ways forward, we help our students grow, and we free ourselves as teachers to be what we've always wanted to be: wildly creative.

A BRIEF HISTORY OF NEARLY EVERYTHING (OR, AT LEAST, OF CURRICULUM IN AMERICA)

Before we get into an example of the actual way this talk of dualism-rejecting-yet-highly-rigorous-creativity looks in real time, let's take a short roller coaster ride to the seeds of curriculum development in America, about a hundred years ago. It's important to set the stage before our push toward creativity can rev its engine fully. So take a breath, grab a handful of popcorn, and turn up the Bruce Springsteen. (Disclaimer: You may feel as though you're reading the education news of today, rather than a hundred years ago.)

Essentially a quarterback's playbook for education in America, the *Report of the Committee of Ten* (National Educational Association, 1894) tried to unify education across the country (ironically, quite similar to what we're seeing currently). The members of the committee often unanimously agreed on methods, contents, and modes of curriculum and of teaching. However, in their report and in the subsequent reports from each subject-matter conference, there is a glaring absence: the *why* of education and schooling. That is, these reports and agendas were content to consider the methods and means by which certain desired outcomes could be obtained through the use of the public school system. If the *Report of the Committee of Ten* were a television commercial today, its jingle might be: *Keep it the same, let's all agree; we don't know exactly why, but you teach like me.* While the initial report (1894) made huge progress in defining what was important for all students to learn and be able to do, its rigidity spawned the soon-to-become-irrevocable power of standards.

Ten years later, a Charles Darwin–obsessed researcher named G. Stanley Hall (1905) offered some pretty awful views about schools and students, including disparaging comments about female students and about how everything a student would ever do was genetically predetermined. But Hall's saving grace is in a series of comments he made in response to the committee's report: "There is no more wild, free, vigorous growth of the forest, but everything is in pots or rows like a rococo garden" (p. 509). In lamenting the loss of children's ability to be active in their schools, Hall (1905) also claimed that education had become nothing more than "factory work to the pupil" (p. 509). Hall's sentiments beg the question: Can schools be rigorous without being rigid in their practice?

Diane Ravitch (2000), in *Left Back*, argues that at the end of the 19th century, two camps emerged regarding the nature of the real purpose of education, led by educational theorists Herbert Spencer and Lester Frank Ward. Spencer sought to establish a system of public education in which "utility" became the key purpose; the question of how a student should be educated would be answered by what that student was likely to do in her or his life. Spencer's notion was problematic in that it supported the status quo of the class structure in America. In other words, why teach the children of a bricklayer the intricacies of literature if they would grow up to be manual laborers like their parents? In contrast, Ward saw education as a tool for *all* students, one that would enable every child—regardless of class—to be offered the same opportunity and possibility within the context of a democratic society. "The main purpose of education, Ward argued, was to equalize society by diffusing knowledge and what he called 'directive intelligence' to all. He literally believed that knowledge was power" (p. 29). Is the debate any different now than it was at the turn of the last century? Is there a choice between education as an emancipatory process, one that enlightens and empowers all students, or education as a utilitarian endeavor, one that simply prepares students for what they're going to *do* next in life?

A synthesis of standards and creativity pushes past the *what* of materials and methods alone and gets into complexity, genuine student involvement, and authentic learning. Such a synthesis also involves seeing education as a journey of enjoyment and exploration rather than a utilitarian process that proceeds from step to step in an orderly fashion. The curriculum battles of a hundred years ago are still relevant and active today, though the faces and names have changed. How can we now infuse the *what*—the testing and the standards—with the joyful, playful curiosity of the *why*? In essence, how can we teach and learn within a framework of standards while also being playfully creative and wildly contemplative?

MOVING FORWARD (THE CROWD GOES WILD)

Complexity and creativity enjoy walking hand-in-hand. They're like a couple, madly in love, that sometimes has nasty fights. But mostly, they smile and pass notes and sometimes are caught kissing in the hallways. Neither complexity nor creativity agrees to easy compromises, making both obstinate—yet interdependent—characteristics of authentic learning. In my own childhood, I believed with all the fervor I had that there was a very strict boundary between one thing and another. Everything was black or white: How could there be shades? This type of rigidity allowed for no function of creativity, no ability to consider complexities and nuances. Something either *was* one way or it wasn't. I hadn't yet learned of the beautiful nature of two little words: *what if?*

For example, let's take a basic principle that I learned as a child and tease it out with *what if*. The rule: Stealing is wrong. Then I saw the magnificent production of *Les Misérables* on a study-abroad program in London when I was a junior in college. Jean Valjean! He stole, but it was only for the purpose of saving a life—of obtaining

food in order to live. Is this really so completely wrong? Is the desire to live actually bad? What if a mother or a father stole something because their child needed
it desperately in order to survive? Would I say this was evil? When the curtain fell
on *Les Misérables*, I remained in my seat in the nose-bleed section and realized that
something in my thinking would forever be changed. My mind was beginning to
see complexity where it had always assumed categorization.

There are not simply two paths. As stated in *The Mindful Teacher* (Shirley &
MacDonald, 2009), there are *only* imperfect ways forward, and, indeed, there have
only been imperfect theories offered in the past regarding how to change our schools
and our teachers. It seems an especially prescient lesson that we have deigned to
learn in the past but need desperately to realize in the present.

A call to creativity, then, can be centered on the notion that everything we do
in schools and what has resulted from the push toward standards and testing is not
simply all bad. There have been good outcomes from the rigorous ways in which
we have challenged our students and in how administrators and policymakers
have challenged us teachers. However, to use a more common phrase, it is high
time to dirty up the water a bit and deal with the complexities of what is at stake:
not simply test scores, but students' attitudes toward learning, involvement in
their own education, and power as people of a free and democratic society. We can
no longer afford to accept tired clichés and dualisms. The best ways forward from
here involve the complexities of multiple voices, multiple methods, and multiple
materials. And what better way to enter into this conversation than through the
means of creativity?

A MICROCOSM FOR THE MARRIAGE OF STANDARDS AND CREATIVITY (MODEL LESSON: THE BOSTON PHOTOGRAPH)

So let's dive right in with the big question: *How?* I want to introduce an example
of a lesson that is highly creative but also addresses key standards. (For the actual
assignment, see Appendix A.) I have used the following lesson with students in my
English classrooms, from grade 7 on through to college-level Rhetorical Analysis.
At each level, the lesson has been met with enthusiasm by a wide range of learners,
from students in an alternative school, to honors-level students, to students in a
juvenile detention facility. Across the board, the lesson evokes students' authentic
thinking and forces them to step into others' shoes. I will give an overview of the
lesson, including what you might say and how you might introduce it, and then I
will comment on the student work and the connections to both standards and to
creativity.

This lesson plan focuses on a historical event that took place in Boston in July
1975. At that time, lower-income housing areas were widely known to be neglected
by fire and police officials, and so many of the apartment complexes were long over-
due for safety changes and additions. The lesson uses one of the actual photographs

taken at the scene of a fire. Your students will be able to view the photograph—though it must be said that it is graphic in nature. (Before reading my description of the lesson, it may help to briefly flip to Appendix A and view the handout there.)

First, as students enter the classroom, it helps to have desks already arranged into groups of three or four. If you only have long tables, you can group chairs together, or you can push the tables to the side of the classroom and use the chairs alone.

As students enter, I recommend leaving the board completely blank. Then, when all have entered and are seated in their groups, silently walk up to the board and write the words "THE BOSTON PHOTOGRAPH" in large block capital letters.

The words will begin to engage students. Do not yet respond to any questions. Take a moment, look at your students, then turn back to the board and write the following date: "JULY 22, 1975." By remaining silent, you will already be engaging students' creativity. They will start to ask themselves questions; they will wonder why you are writing these things on the board.

Wait another moment, walk around the room a few paces, and then return to the board. Finally, at the very top, write the words (in very, very small print—but still large enough to be deciphered if students *really* try): "a true story."

Then turn back to your class and tell them the story of the July 22, 1975, fire. (The actual details of what happened are included on the first page of the assignment, below the photograph.) You have not yet handed out the actual assignment to students. Instead, you are practicing the ancient and beautiful art of storytelling, engaging your students in a powerful, poignant, and tragic true story of what happened that fateful day. None of your students will ever have heard of this day's events in Boston. It helps to go slowly—do not rush the details. Discuss the fear that Diana and Tiare probably felt. When you share how photographer Stanley Forman climbed onto the back of the truck, preface it by juxtaposing his decision to try to get a better picture against the tragedy of someone in utter danger. When you discuss how close Bob O'Neil is to reaching the two people, reach your hand out, as if you are Bob O'Neil yourself, and you can almost . . . *almost* . . . almost . . . reach them. And when you share what happened to the fire escape, show the emotion and shock and horror on your own face.

Then, do not say anything more about the actual scene. Instead, say the following (or something like it in your own words and style): "Two hours later, Stanley Forman walks into the editorial board meeting of the *Boston Herald American*, the photos he has taken in hand. One of the women has died. She was pronounced dead at the scene. Forman hands these photos depicting a real death—someone's tragic fall from an *old* fire escape [stress this fact, then pause]. Look to your right and left. The people you are sitting with are your editorial board. Your group is the members of the board of the *Boston Herald American*. Your paper is going to print in less than 1 hour. You have 25 minutes to make one single decision: Will you print the photos?"

Pause for a moment to allow students to register the information you have told them, along with their mission. Then tell students that you will now pass out one of the actual photos Forman took, along with a written description of all the details of the story you just shared. Tell the students that the photo is shocking, and instruct them to take this seriously, as this is real human life—not movies, not television, and not make-believe. And their decision is just as serious.

While you are passing around the first two sheets (it works well to have the first two sheets printed two-sided), students will begin to ask you, "What really happened? Did they print the photos? What happened to the little girl?" Tell your students that you cannot answer any questions yet. After each group has made its decision and presented and defended it to the rest of the "staff" (i.e., their class-mates), you will then share the actual decision and its results.

Give students 5 or 10 minutes to examine the photograph and to read the written account of the story you have just told them. (They have now received the details of the story twice—once orally and once reading independently or with group mem-bers). Instruct students to turn their sheets over and go through the requirements and guidelines of these 25 minutes of their editorial board meetings. Be sure to be clear, and stress how important and *historical* their decision really will be.

Allow students the 25 minutes to work. You will find that this block of time will make you feel wonderful because students will start debating, talking, sharing, and defending their own ideas. I have done this lesson with 19 different classes, and it always evokes emotions, opinions, ideas, and creative thinking. Students will begin to wonder what will happen if they print the photos. They will feel differently about the image you've given them. Some will wonder about the little girl and about the older woman's family. Some will think about the newspaper itself. Some will claim that the paper's ultimate goal is business—to make money. Others will claim that the newspaper's goal is to challenge the status quo.

As these discussions continue in each group, listen closely, because what your students talk so passionately about here can help direct further activities and assign-ments and projects you might consider. Also, this lesson is a powerful lead-in to discussions of poverty and wealth, heroism, materialism, and other themes that are widely explored in literature—both fiction and nonfiction.

As you go from group to group, continue to ask probing questions, and show how difficult this choice really is. This is an incredibly important addendum to today's lesson: that while schools and societies often want to teach a right/wrong dichotomy, there are frequently far more complicated questions at stake. This kind of creative and critical thinking does wonders for students. Not only will it make them a bit uncomfortable (which is very, very good!), it will begin to open their minds to the possibility that on their own, they do not possess all the answers. They will be forced to seek others' ideas, to gather more information, and yet still make their own decisions in the end.

Once group time is finished, create a list on the board of which groups will present and defend their decisions. I find that having an order before beginning to share allows the presentation and discussion to go more smoothly, rather than stopping after each group and waiting once you've asked, "Okay . . . who wants to go next?" Momentum is aided by a continuing discussion of each group's decisions. Remember, as the teacher, you do not need to continually insert yourself; groups can see on the board when it's their turn, and they can automatically rise, walk to the front of the classroom, and present their ideas.

Do not rush this segment. This is where a lot of learning happens. Students are presenting their own ideas and learning how to defend them. They are also engaging with the rest of the class and responding to questions about and criticisms of their decisions. This is creative work and growth at its best.

Every once in a while, if the conversation slows, it helps to throw in your own ideas, play devil's advocate, or suggest a question that has not been considered. I also like to keep a running tally on one side of the board as to the final decision groups make: To print or not to print?

Once all groups have presented, you will find that students are very eager to hear the "real" decision and its consequences. Again, don't rush this. It can help increase their interest to say things like, "Well, we don't have much time. I'll share what really happened tomorrow" or "Does it really matter what *actually* happened? Why?" Again, these are small ways to keep students engaged and still get them thinking creatively about what they've been learning and why they want to know— indeed, *need to know*—what really happened.

First share orally the newspaper's decision and the consequences of Forman's photographs, then pass out the third sheet. This last sheet is the written account you have already told them, but it also includes two questions for deeper creative and critical thinking. These can be discussed and written about in groups, done as homework, or completed independently in class, depending on your classroom procedures and time allotments.

I find this lesson helpful to use toward the start of a school year. It gets students very engaged and also helps them to begin to see that words, pictures, and decisions about how they are used have incredible significance and impacts in the real world. Additionally, students will now have assumed the role of an actual editorial board—thus, they have been faced with a complicated decision, and they have been forced to work with a group to come to a consensus and defend their decision.

This lesson involves highly creative, empathetic, and critical thinking. It hits many standards, including those addressing the need for students in an English class to defend their ideas, use written expression to make and support an argument, work cooperatively within a group, and communicate orally and argue their case. Versions of these general standards will be in every single state's book and included in any talk of standardization. However, instead of completing a rote activity or doing something that fails to engage your students' emotions and empathy, you will have used a historical event that has demanded their attention, and you will have forced them to sit in an uncomfortable position and yet still act.

This lesson can have a variety of offshoots for further work. You can ask students to write a one- or two-page creative memoir of what Tiare's life is like 30 years later. How does she cope with knowing her image has been published along with that of the woman she was with, who died? Or you can have students examine poverty and wealth and whether fire codes and other such important safety measures are still neglected in lower-income housing areas today. Perhaps some of your students live in lower-income housing areas. Or maybe some of them are wealthy and live in large, beautiful homes. In either case, you can ask them to explore, in writing, how they think their social class affects their ways of thinking and their worldviews. Ask them to consider how money influences the decisions and actions of individuals, of groups, and of government agencies. You can segue into a novel such as *The Great Gatsby* (Fitzgerald, 1925/2001) as you discuss money and its influence. Or you can dive into an authentic research project, asking students to create surveys to use with other students in the building as they question the role of class in obtaining adequate housing and safety standards.

Essentially, there are limitless possibilities for where to go from here. Lessons like "The Boston Photograph" can also be included in a creative writing unit you already have. It might be added as a way to focus on a very real, human, and tragic story that is representative of a whole host of issues. In short, a lesson like this does exactly what good literature is crafted to do: It uses one story to share many; it uses the emotion of one painful experience to elucidate a universal theme of living we might otherwise miss. And it allows for creativity to thrive amid a culture of standards, whereby important skills aren't ignored, but instead are given an environment in which to be practiced *through* creativity rather than through a more traditional approach.

GUIDING QUESTIONS

1. In what ways could an activity like "The Boston Photograph" work in your classroom? Could it tie into a unit you already teach, or a poem or short story you already explore with students?
2. Do you feel pressure to adhere to a rigid curriculum, high-stakes test preparation, or dualistic thinking? When do you feel these pressures most? When do you feel them least?
3. An activity: Take 10 minutes (I know! Your minutes are precious! But really, *please* do this—okay, okay, take 7 minutes. Fine . . . last offer: 6 minutes) and briefly record all the reasons why you first wanted to become an English teacher. Just write your heart out for those 6 minutes, and then reread it.
4. Do you still believe what you wrote for item 3? Are your reasons for teaching still the same? If not, what are they now?

CHAPTER 2

Reading and Responding Like a Human Being

Outside our schools, students are not much different from us teachers. Their hearts beat fast when they're nervous, as do ours. They're exhaustibly confused by relationships, as are we. They love the feel of Butterfinger ice cream on their tongues just as much as we do. But when our students enter the classroom, commands from the hierarchal powers-that-be filter through our minds and we often forget that—like us—our students are human beings, too. How can we appeal to their humanity? How can we awaken their souls to the power of words in a way that also supports standards?

RUBRICS WITH HOLES? A CASE IN POINT

Many years ago, as a student teacher just outside of Boston, I recall walking into Mr. John Robinson's classroom with a head full of nervous possibilities and incredibly sweaty armpits. *How would students react to me? Would they see my nervousness? Would discussions about literature and writing proceed as rapturously as I had hoped?* The questions circled my mind as Mr. Robinson slowly helped me take over the classes.

I learned much in those 5 months of student teaching, but my most valuable lesson occurred after the students had left the school building. Mr. Robinson was teaching me how to go through a student's thesis essay, mark it up, and grade it. He showed me the rubric for the essay and talked about how important it is to highlight some errors while letting others go so that a student doesn't become overwhelmed by a paper that has writing across the entire thing. However, Mr. Robinson's pen certainly couldn't stay still for long, and I watched as he made powerful insertions and comments in the margins and across the text. It was beautiful—and even now, as I recall that first dance with marking up a student text, Billy Collins's (2002) insightful poem "Marginalia" comes to mind.

After modeling the process of marking up and grading a student essay several times, Mr. Robinson gave me a look that held a smile and said, "Ready to begin?" I nodded, picked up a blue Uniball pen, 0.7 thickness, and turned the title page on the essay—the first of thousands that were to come.

After an hour or so of grading side-by-side, I heard Mr. Robinson heave a heavy sigh, cap his pen, and lean back in his chair. He looked like he was a bit distraught or as though he had perhaps eaten too much garlic. Since there were no cloves anywhere in sight of our grading table in Room 106, I assumed the former to be true.

"What?" I asked him in a rather noncommittal fashion.

"It's this essay," he said, and then passed it my way. "Read it."

I read the entire essay and was struck by the precision of the language, the way the student had used the correct number of examples from the text, cited them correctly, and organized the work seamlessly according to the rubric and the general requirements of a strong critical-analytical essay. I smiled, thinking this was an easy one to grade: A+, no questions asked.

But why was Mr. Robinson distraught over such an essay?

I let the question linger in my eyes before I gave it life in my voice.

"Read it once more," he replied.

So I did. The second time through I realized that something was missing. Indeed, the rubric had been followed perfectly. The word choice was precise, the citing was perfect, the case was duly proven. But it was . . . it was . . . *too perfect*. In short, it had no authenticity in it.

Finally, he looked at me and said, "That essay has no soul."

Now, you may be reading this wondering what point there is in discussing something as indefinable and vague as *soul*. However, I would venture that there's a part of you that innately understands exactly what my supervising teacher meant when he said those words. Indeed, in my own experience teaching at three levels, I saw my share of these kinds of essays. The students followed the rubric. They could check off the requirements. They could earn their As for the work. However, the question came to annoy me no end: *What is at stake in these essays?*

Standards can be incredibly valuable tools. They can enhance the way we function with students, and they can provide clarity to students about the steps they must take to learn important skills and master content. However, when standards outmaneuver meaning, we've lost our way. The *why* and the *how* of what we do are always just as important as the *what is expected*. When we focus only on the results, it is indeed very possible that we end up with student work that checks off every single box required yet still lacks the less easily found inspiration, authentic learning, and growth that we so passionately hope for as teachers.

IT'S OKAY TO SAY "SOUL" IN SCHOOL

In their powerful article "Starting with the Soul," Sam Intrator and Robert Kunzman (2006) describe what they perceive to be a deficient area in teacher growth and sustainability. "We believe that effective professional development and the powerful teaching it can cultivate require an inversion of Maslow's pyramid. We need to begin with the *soul* of the enterprise, the passion and purpose that animate teachers' ongoing commitment to students and learning. Too many of our conversations about effective teaching focus on content, teaching methods, and learning outcomes" (p. 38). Their contention here is that something less well defined and much less talked about is often neglected in the area of professional development for teachers. While Maslow's hierarchy suggests that humans care first and foremost about essential needs such as food, shelter, and clothing, the authors invert Maslow's claims in the area of education to state that the opposite is true: that teachers first need to begin with "the soul of the enterprise" in teaching and move on from there to specific tools for teachers and for teacher growth.

The edited volume *Authenticity in Teaching* (Cranton, 2006) includes five provocative and engaging pieces that explore the ideology of authenticity and its possible applications to teaching. In one of the articles, John Dirkx (2006) states that "We foster authenticity in our teaching by connecting with a deeper sense of who we are. Doing this represents a kind of soul work, in which we attend to and work imaginatively with the emotions and feelings associated with our teaching, and the images that come to animate these emotions and feelings" (p. 31).

So if teachers need an infusion of "soul" in order to sustain their practice, wouldn't the same be true for students? In fact, researchers Ingersoll and Smith (2004) provide a harrowing statistic about teacher retention: Almost half of all teachers quit the profession within their first 3 years. One factor for many of these teachers is the relentless pressure on performing in a data-driven enterprise, rather than one that encourages creativity, soul, and passion. So new teachers can try out the profession, and if they come up against too many walls, they quit.

But our students don't have the same options. They can't quit. (At least, not until they're 16.) And if we really care about them, we don't want them to quit. We want *school* to cease to be a bad word. We want *school* to conjure up joy, not fear; expression, not suppression; growth, not memorization.

For such a change to occur, we must start to allow ourselves as teachers to use a word like *soul*. We've got to start looking at student writing and allow our minds to recognize, "Hey, that essay hits all the points of the rubric, but it doesn't seem like the writer actually learned much or interacted with the text. Why the heck is that?"

When we emphasize standards alone, or when we reduce any enterprise to its most common denominators, we miss out on all the beautiful scribbles in the margins. In short, we lose the poetry in order to obey the rules. But how can we offer methods of responding to literature that don't just generate student writing that is personally distant from the text and does not produce authentic learning?

When using a novel in class, it's often helpful to use brief essays or short stories before, during, and after reading the novel. One of the books I love reading with my 11th-graders is Zora Neale Hurston's (1937/2001) *Their Eyes Were Watching God*. Love! Marriage! Fear! Self-esteem! Breaking boundaries! The book is chock-full of all the themes 11th-graders are texting about with one another anyway. But to help them access a book like Hurston's, it's helpful to allow students to use the skill of critical analysis in a creative way: by critically analyzing their own culture and themselves.

A brief assignment that explores marriage, like "Love and Marriage?" (Appendix B), is one way to help students to think critically in a creative, open-ended format. What 11th-grader has not thought, even a little, about marriage? Even if they're vehemently against marriage, they've still thought enough to claim: *No way, home slice, not for me!* So in conjunction with Hurston's book (or most novels that explore themes of love and marriage), you can use an essay like "What I Wish I Had Known About Marriage," by Kristin Armstrong (2006). The essay gets students interested in the theme, but it's not too long. Then allow students the space to think and write openly about themselves, their own desires, and the culture they see on television, in their homes, and in school. The questions for this assignment aren't closed, and there is distinctly no right answer to any of them. They aren't *either–or* questions, and they will generate classroom discussion, debate, and interest.

You can refer back to an assignment like this as you read through *Their Eyes Were Watching God*, and you can use what students write here as a way to test whether Janie's experiences in the novel are changing the ways that your students are thinking about themselves and their own goals. Using a sheet like Appendix B helps students to think critically, but it doesn't come across as a rigid, five-paragraph thesis essay that will immediately close the door to many students' interests. And those students who will work hard to complete it will often do so without a sense of inner motivation; instead, they will leave their souls at the door and write *only* according to a rubric instead of their authentic experiences and ideas.

Once certain writing assignments, essays, and debates and discussions have been held, students (and you!) may be excited or terrified by this next step. Quite simply, it's what Parker Palmer (1998) highlights in his groundbreaking book *The Courage to Teach*: "Bad teachers distance themselves from the subject they are teaching—and in the process, from their students. Good teachers join self and subject and students in the fabric of life. Good teachers possess a capacity for connectedness" (p. 11). Palmer claims that insecurity and fear of vulnerability can cripple teachers. Ultimately, he asserts that good teaching involves the ability to self-examine and be truthful about one's own strengths and weaknesses.

Whoa.

When I first read Palmer as a new teacher, I realized my teaching wasn't honest enough. I wanted my students to engage with material. I wanted literature and writing to change the way my students saw themselves and the world around them. Yet I wasn't willing to allow for the same transformation within myself. Simply put, if I was ever going to interest students in the material, I would have to also show my own interest in the text. National Book Award–winning essayist and novelist Gore Vidal once said, "If you want to be interesting, be interested." And that means one scary, terrifying, nightmarish thing: *vulnerability*.

With a book like *Their Eyes Were Watching God*, the chance for just this kind of teacher-modeled vulnerability is ripe. In the novel, Janie gets involved in a series of awful relationships. Who among us—teachers, administrators, and policymakers alike—hasn't walked those same broken roads from time to time? And every one of our students has or will walk these same roads of trial and error when it comes to relationships. It becomes more and more ludicrous to expect students—and teachers!—to read such a vulnerable, moving novel and then respond to it as though we are automatons, generating essays cooked medium or medium-well with the heat of a rubric. Instead, we need to allow ourselves as teachers—and allow our students—to see the Janie inside of us, too.

I decided to talk with my students about a time when I wanted a girlfriend to fill a hole within myself—believing, as in the film *Jerry Maguire*, that another person "completes" us. I ultimately found this to be false, of course, and I share with my students how I, too, am like Janie in this way. But then I share with them the story of my wife, Jennifer, and how I knew that I wanted to try to love her in a way that helped me grow as a person. I use an assignment like "Considering Janie, Considering You, Considering Love" (Appendix C) to get students thinking about their perceptions of love and relationships, which includes the beautiful poem by W. B. Yeats, "When You Are Old" (1893/2000). I also tell my students the story of when I first told Jennifer that I loved her and how I memorized Yeats's poem to share with my wife-to-be. I share how nervous I felt and how I had hoped the words would not leave me high and dry as I professed my love. My obvious vulnerability in this story helps my students feel more comfortable being vulnerable, too. It gets them thinking, *Hey, maybe I can let my soul run around a bit inside this classroom.* . . . In sharing myself, and my own emotional responses to Hurston's novel, I also begin to model for students what reading and responding to literature is essentially all about: connection between the messages and emotions within a text and the turmoil and tension we discover within ourselves. We'll get deeper into the idea of teachers and vulnerability later on when we discuss creative writing as a tool for teachers as well as students to learn at deeper levels, but for now, suffice it to say that authentic learning can never occur with literature unless vulnerability is present. It's a pestering fact that we cannot skirt. As teachers, when we model authentic interaction with a text, we show students how to let their guard down and to begin to let characters, messages, ideas, and possibilities penetrate their hearts, too.

My 7th-graders and I read Lorraine Hansberry's (1959/2004) Pulitzer Prize–winning play, *A Raisin in the Sun*. It is a remarkably moving account of one African American family trying to learn what the American Dream means for them and whether it is possible in a society whose foundational stones are still set upon racism and inequality. It's difficult to read through and perform a play like this without challenging students to see their own connections with the themes. "Something Left to Love?" (Appendix D) is an example of how students can be encouraged to personally connect to a text while also unlocking the theme in preparation for rewriting a powerful scene as it applies to their own lives. An activity like this can be used with any novel, play, short story, or poem. Students are encouraged to annotate—a skill that is foundational to interacting with texts—and then to explore theme and tone so as to critique the way a meaning is transmitted through language. In an activity like this, all kinds of high-level thinking are occurring. But students' personal connection with the text, and the rewriting of material to reflect their own situations and people they know and love, makes *Raisin* even more powerful for them.

Another highly valuable tool when responding to literature with our souls is the Socratic Seminar, made popular by Mortimer Adler's (1998) book *The Paideia Proposal*. In brief, the Socratic (or Paideia) Seminar is a method of discussion whereby the idea of "right answers" is removed from a teacher's objectives. In asking students to respond to a text, the underlying principle is to back up opinions and claims with evidence. This is an excellent tool for developing critical thinkers. Students cite lines from text and also use examples from their own experiences and from their culture to lend credibility to their arguments. Personal connections are encouraged, and the questions are designed to be open-ended, while the teacher remains almost silent during the discussion—more a facilitator than an active participant. Socrates believed that truth could be found by constant questioning and by using evidence and experiences to support what one finds. For an overview of the Socratic Seminar, see "Paideia (or Socratic) Seminar" (Appendix E). This is the document I give my students when introducing the idea of the seminar. We read through it together, and then we discuss what this kind of dialogue is like. "Socratic Seminar: *The Skin I'm In* by Sharon G. Flake" (Appendix F) is an assignment I use with my 7th-graders in preparation for a Socratic Seminar on the novel *The Skin I'm In* by Sharon G. Flake (1998). The three questions here are designed to get students interested in sharing their ideas, but they must have some support during this process. That support, however, can be highly creative and interactive while also helping students learn to be critical. In using Socratic Seminars, I have seen many students change their ideas or stances after heated and lively discussions around a text. Indeed, I have occasionally changed my own opinions after hearing my students respond!

Using the Socratic Seminar, including space for personal connection to the text, and encouraging students to respond with their souls intact as they read and consider the *meaning* of the characters and ideas they discover—all of these are valuable tools for helping students to authentically learn (and remember!) what they experience and read. However, there's no way around the fact that the middle and secondary English classroom is, indeed, an incubating chamber for teaching the critical-analytical thesis essay. The skill of critiquing language and literature is essential for students; indeed, it carries over to other areas of life. However, the problem we face as teachers is: *How can we help students creatively critique literature?* In other words, how can we challenge students to learn the difficult skills of literary analysis while keeping their souls intact and—*gasp*—helping their souls grow?

CREATIVE LITERARY ANALYSIS
(OR WHY I LOVE TOM CRUISE, JACK NICHOLSON, AND DEMI MOORE)

I'll never forget the way I felt when I first watched the film *A Few Good Men* (Brown & Reiner, 1992). I sat in complete attention and awe as I watched the final 30 minutes, where Tom Cruise's character (a young wet-behind-the-ears lawyer) passionately interrogates Jack Nicholson's character (an older, highly decorated Marine officer who commands the U.S. troops at Guantanamo Bay) on the stand. Cruise is relentless, citing specific evidence, using emotional pleas, making connections, and accounting for other "texts" that support his ultimate goal of exposing the ruthlessness of Nicholson's character. In short, Cruise does everything we desperately hope our students will do when writing a critical-analytical essay.

So before I introduce the first thesis essay of the year to my students, I show them the final 30 minutes of *A Few Good Men*. I prepare them by claiming that as writers, they, too, are like Cruise. They can never separate passion and personhood from what they write—even if the result is going to be a highly critical text. In teaching our students that the "I" must always be removed when performing analysis, I believe we make a grave error. Granted, we cannot lean so deeply into the personal that the text itself ceases to have its own identity, but our analysis proves to be far deeper and more meaningful if we allow the self to come in and play, too. Cruise's character demonstrates this balance perfectly: His passion is evident, his opinions are bold, and the personal reasons that lead him to argue his case so powerfully are undeniable. But still, the critical backbone and evidence are articulate and precise.

After my students and I watch the film clip, I try my best to reframe the thesis essay less as a necessary evil and more as an opportunity for them to passionately connect to a text and argue their case. Using the stance of a lawyer, students are in good company, with characters like the one Cruise plays and fictional heroes like Atticus Finch. That is our ideal for how students will creatively and passionately argue their case. Thus, in keeping with this kind of tone throughout the thesis essay, I use scaffolding aids like "The Marriage of Passion and Purpose" (Appendix G). This outline helps my 11th-grade students find quotes for their thesis essays, strikes a tone that is authentic for me as a teacher (finding your authentic tone with your students is almost as important as the assignments themselves!), and reminds my students of our work with the film *A Few Good Men*.

Prior to working on an activity like Appendix G, my students and I will already have gone through a full class period of asking the question: *What makes a good thesis statement?* It's a very important lesson, as it sets up expectations, but is, I hope, creative in its process rather than a top-down, worksheet-driven, or rubric-style delivery. The essential goals for the lesson are that students will be able to effectively revise a thesis statement to incorporate (1) a passionate argument that takes a stance and (2) clear, bold language.

As students enter the room, they are given a dry-erase marker (or chalk). Once some brief introductory remarks are made, students are asked to write their thesis statement on whiteboard (or chalkboard). Music will be playing as the students do this (from *Good Morning, Vietnam* or *Rudy* or another favorite film soundtrack). I remind students of the two keys that I am looking for in a strong thesis (which we've seen in full force while viewing *A Few Good Men*): a passionate argument and clear, bold language. Then I ask each student to choose two thesis statements from the board that are not their own and copy them onto a sheet of blank paper. I encourage students to choose their statements from different areas of the board. I then give them 3 or 4 minutes to proofread the statements on their page and revise them for the two specific qualities we've discussed at some length: (1) an argument that has an edge and can be passionately defended or proven and (2) clarity of language and meaning.

When students have finished their revisions, I ask for volunteers to share with the class the first statement they chose and their ideas for improvements. If any other student has also chosen that statement, I will also give him or her ample time to contribute. As students make suggestions, I revise the lines on the board. After proceeding through three or four thesis statements, I ask each student to go to the statement he or she chose as a second example and make the suggested revisions on the board (if a number of students chose the same thesis, that's fine—they will all need to talk about the changes they made and decide on the best ones).

When the students sit down, I lead a discussion on changes in three or four of the statements (more or less, depending on time and need evidenced in the students by their remarks). As a class, we will decide if the changes are necessary and helpful. Finally, students go to the board a third time and rewrite their *own* thesis statements. During this time, I also float around the class and help students individually. Throughout the experience, students are getting up and sitting down, seeing their statements on the board, watching revisions take place, and being constantly reminded (by a pestering Mr. Reynolds) that boldness and passion are just as important as evidence and specific claims.

At the conclusion of this exercise, students write down their new thesis statements—or, if they believe that their original thesis statements were already strong, they prepare to passionately defend why no changes have been made (thereby creating another, albeit brief, thesis experience!).

As teachers, we can help students respond in creative and passionate ways to literature. By the overuse of rubrics, data-driven methods, and traditional critical-analytical essay preparations, we may end up alienating our students from a process that is deeply personal and must remain so if their writing is to possess great clarity, insight, and soul. This is why in every essay I assign my students, especially the critical-analytical thesis essay, I encourage students to personally connect to the texts they are critiquing. One of my writing mentors, Nancy Nies, once told me, "Involvement precedes interest." There is great truth in this statement, and if we don't encourage students to become involved with a text, their interest will wane. And if their interest wanes, we'll receive a great many thesis essays (or other written responses) that may check off quite a few boxes on a rubric but possess very little soul.

After all, literature in all its genres and forms—poetry, novels, plays, stories, memoirs, and more—is created in incredible emotion, vulnerability, desire, and meaning. Therefore, to ask students to relate to literature without also incorporating these cornerstones is like asking a thirsty man to quench his thirst by merely *thinking* about water but never actually feeling the cool liquid course down his throat.

NONTRADITIONAL BOOK RESPONSES AND THE THESIS ESSAY, REVISITED

As an alternative to the thesis essay in responding to a full-length book, students might be challenged to complete a project like "My Ideal Country" (Appendix H), which asks them to respond to Livia Bitton-Jackson's (1999) Holocaust memoir, *I Have Lived a Thousand Years,* in a highly creative yet also rigorous way. I used the assignment with my 7th-graders but it can easily be modified for higher or lower grade levels, and it can be changed to meet the needs of any book that explores suffering and pain in the face of corruption, evil dictatorships, and oppressive powers. This assignment challenges students to produce writing of very high quality, persuasion, critical thinking, and creative ways of solving problems that are both current and perennial. In considering their own ideal countries, students must get beyond surface thinking and examine the flaws of Nazi Germany, which they are familiar with after reading Bitton-Jackson's powerful account. Skills like thinking critically, making connections, analyzing the text, conceptualizing ideas, applying theory to practical situations, and synthesizing information are all inherent in an assignment like this. In many ways, such work accomplishes a lot of what the traditional thesis essay seeks to accomplish, but in a more creative and interactive way. Added skill building and practice can be included in this assignment by asking students to make presentations about their countries (public speaking, listening skills) or even by using the countries created in a classroom to run a mock world for a few weeks (or, if you are highly organized, for the duration of the academic year). How would these newly created countries interact with one another? What problems might emerge? How would they trade? Would the rights of citizens in one country cause the rights of those in another to be limited or infringed upon for any reasons? In other words, creative responses to literature like this one can be as complex and detailed as you would like them to become, or as limited and focused as your curriculum has time to afford.

Since we've broached the subject of the thesis essay in this chapter, it seems fitting to include mention of one other assignment that helps to teach the essentials of making a claim, supporting that claim with specific evidence, and then relating those essential understandings to self and the wider world around us. I have used the thesis essay assignment "I Am Because" (Appendix I) with my freshman composition classes at the college level. This assignment challenges students to consider what forces have shaped their identities, and, in so doing, the scaffold of the rhetorical triangle is immensely helpful. Students are often excited when they learn about ethos (credibility), logos (logic), and pathos (emotion), since it begins to give them a framework for how messages in media, literature, advertisements, films, and even other people try to persuade them to think, feel, or act out certain ideas. There are a number of creative ways to teach the skill of using the rhetorical triangle—including asking students to create commercials in the form of skits in which they must employ all three rhetorical tools—but this thesis essay (Appendix I) has been the most moving for me and my students to work through.

An example of a similar kind of thesis essay that asks students to explore their own lives, decisions, and perceptions for a younger classroom is included in "Do You Live Like a Crab?" (Appendix J). I created this assignment to help address a recurring theme that I saw with my 7th-graders—namely, the notion that doing well or receiving good grades is somehow "not cool." Additionally, the "Crab" thesis essay challenges students to consider the influences of the people around them and therefore helps them begin to distinguish their own dreams, goals, and ideas from what others say they should want and do. Thesis essays like these last two examples teach me much about my students and allow them a space to consider who they are in light of the influences around them. The assignments embody creative analysis that enables students to learn skills that we teachers can find on any list of state or national standards, and yet students will rise to the occasion to incorporate their souls into such assignments.

CONCLUSIONS

When we remember that we read and love literature and writing because it speaks to us and moves us deeply, we also reclaim that truth for our students. Skill building, high standards, and critical thinking can all grow with creative assignments and assessments just as much as with traditional methods.

Our students are not all that different from ourselves. They long to be seen for who they are, and they long to be communicated with and related to in a way that honors their humanity. The very things that move us, move them. The very things that terrify us, terrify them. The very things that make us want to laugh ourselves silly—spitting up rivulets of milk mixed in with crumbs of assorted foods—well, yes, these things also make our students laugh themselves silly. After years of cafeteria duty and teachers' lounge lunches, I've come to see that the two locales are irresistibly similar. (One day, I hope that some odd researcher will devise a qualitative study of both entities, comparing the conversations, nonverbal cues, and "rules" inherent to each; until that day, my own anecdotal observations will have to suffice.) Students congregate around their lunch tables, gossiping about who is going out with whom, who farted in class, whose dad left, who has most recently been disrespected or accorded respect by the powers-that-be among their peers. Meanwhile, we teachers huddle in the teachers' lounge, gossiping about who is getting married to (or divorced from) whom; who farted/made some other random, weird, or strange sound/comment in class; whose child is struggling/achieving; who has most recently been disrespected or accorded respect by the powers-that-be among peers or administrators.

In other words, we're pretty similar. Students and teachers alike, we want what's real. We want to know the scoop. We want to talk about emotions. We want to know what's going on in the heart. We want to know about things that make us laugh ourselves silly or cry ourselves dry. As an English teacher, you have that most remarkable of all opportunities: to say to your students, *Yes, I'm a human, too. I once felt like Yeats did. I once hurt like Janie did. I once wept and laughed and cried and tried. I still do.* And in sharing assignments that are both rigorous and creative, both truth-seeking and truth-telling, we free not only our students but also ourselves.

GUIDING QUESTIONS

1. What is most scary about being vulnerable with your students? What kinds of texts have moved you deeply, and how have novels, stories, plays, and poetry played a role in important moments of your life? Which of these stories could you share with your students?
2. How might you use clips from films like *A Few Good Men* to help teach the passionate parts of the critical-analytical essay? What films or songs come to mind that might be beneficial for you to use in your classroom?
3. Can you say the word *soul* without smiling? Why not? Can you discuss an powerful text without thinking about your soul and the deep parts of who you are?
4. Find the text of Mary Oliver's poem "The Journey" (via Google or another search engine). Read the poem aloud to yourself, or to your toilet paper roll, or to a stuffed animal you have not yet thrown away. What voices might you need to leave behind when it comes to including creative ways for students to respond to literature in your classroom?
5. Was there anything in this chapter that did not resonate at all? What ideas or lesson got you excited? Why do you think you reacted strongly either way?
6. Try the following (it will be worthwhile, I promise): On a blank piece of paper, write this sentence starter: If I could respond to texts in any way I wanted with my students, without fear of test scores diminishing, or low evaluations, or awkward glances from my colleagues, I would . . .

Finish with everything that comes to your mind. Allow yourself to freely write all of the creative and goofy and strange ways you'd love to have students respond to the beautiful and poignant literature you read within the walls of your classroom. Then wait a day. When you return to your entry or list of ideas, make at least three of them a reality—no matter how crazy they all are. Consider that your free, creative, and crazy self may help student test scores rise just as much as your traditional, worried, overwhelmed self.

CHAPTER 3

The Play's the Thing: Writing as Creative and Rigorous

DATA-DRIVEN MEASURES for the English classroom often work from the assumption that students can only learn rigorous, effective, and clear writing skills when they're *responding to* texts. In essence, the underlying operational anchor of most standards is that something only comes from something. Another way to articulate this "rule" is to say that students can only grow as writers when they are engaged in analysis and rhetorical criticism regarding poetry, fiction, or nonfiction that is not their own. But what if we interrogate this basic assumption? A hard question emerges: Can students grow just as much as writers—becoming effective communicators of powerful, precise words—by creating their own work rather than (only) analyzing the work of others? By playing with their own words, rather than just analyzing those of others, students can be empowered to write not only with rigor but also with love.

CAN WE DO THIS IN SCHOOL?

The novella project I mentioned in the Introduction was my first real dance with something entirely off-the-wall and not listed on any curriculum guide I could find. It wasn't on the Essential Questions my department chair gave me, and none of my colleagues suggested anything other than an occasional free-write could be included in a literature course at the secondary level. The restraints of test preparation, administrative demands, and skill building drove most of us to constantly claim, *Not enough time!* So I did what anyone would do.

I continued in secret.

The day I introduced the novella assignment to my 11th-graders, I felt an immense giddiness. This goofy happiness could have been the result of one of two things: (1) I felt as though I must have been dreaming to be talking about an assignment that tickled my soul to its core, or (2) it was that nervous delirium that comes just before you consciously realize that you've done something incredibly stupid and may soon be told to get a cardboard box and pack up your desk. Perhaps it was a mixture of both.

In any event, I felt . . . well . . . *freedom*. I was teaching in a public secondary school that had a reputation for high standards, rigorous and organized planning, and highly detailed curriculum guides for all teachers. Certainly, there was little room for deviation from the norm, and even less free time to start a project that would force my students to miss out on some of the "required" assignments and activities. Nonetheless, something inside me suggested that their test scores would be safe—and maybe even improve—with a rigorous *creative* assignment. So I handed out "Losing Sight of the Shore" (Appendix K).

Granted, it's quite heavy on the teacher-speak and there's an awful lot of information on the assignment, but I wanted to model the kind of freedom with which I was asking my students to write. It would be a big project—especially for those students who did not particularly enjoy writing—but I felt that by the time they were finished, with enough freedom and encouragement to be creative and express their ideas through strong, clear, and vivid language, students would be proud of what they had created.

Along the way, I gave my students encouraging notes to keep them writing, like "AAAAAAAHHHHHHH!" (Appendix L), which I used as students were in the brainstorming stage for their novellas. These motivational guides were gleaned from professional writers, authors whose work has been marked by freedom and growth and beautiful stories, such as Anne Lamott (1995) in her book *Bird by Bird* and John Dufresne (2004) in his volume *The Lie That Tells a Truth*. I also wanted my tone to be authentic; I knew that when students recognized that this assignment came straight from my heart to theirs, it had a greater possibility of accomplishing its purposes: to help them gain essential writing skills in a creative way while enhancing their appreciation and even love for the craft of writing.

While many students were skeptical of this assignment, and some thought they could never complete it, most of them produced fine work, and *all* of them had an immense rise in the respect they accorded published authors. For the rest of the academic year, whenever we worked through a novel, students were able to point out lines and discuss decisions the author made in a totally new and fresh way.

And their test scores rose.

So the short answer to the question that heads this section is, *Yes, we can do a novella project in school*. The purpose of this book, however, isn't to merely pass on some assignments I've done and encourage you to copy them—although that is entirely fine and I would perhaps do a small jig if you e-mailed me to say that you are doing the novella project with your students. Instead, my goal is to encourage and challenge you to think about ways you might help your students write creatively, trusting that as you work on creative writing, test scores will not plummet and writing abilities will not disappear. How might you change the novella assignment to match your own passions and interests in the classroom? What kinds of motivational scaffolds might you craft for your students during work on an intense creative project? Might you be silly? Might you be emotionally gripping? Might you be compelling, vulnerable, excited, raving mad, and *alive*? YES. You will be all of those things because, after all, you are a teacher. And what more noble, sacred, and beautiful calling is there in this life? The truth is, you became a teacher because you want to deeply inspire your students *and yourself*. Go ahead, take a risk and start brainstorming some creative writing activities you might use with your students. Even in a literature course.

AN INTERLUDE OF THEORETICAL UNDERPINNING (CUE MOZART)

But why use creative writing as a method in the first place? Why engage students and ourselves in such an endeavor? Just because it may be more fun or entertaining? Just because it might keep students more engaged? Just because it's another way of raising test scores? Yes to those reasons. But yes, as well, to another, and arguably more important, reason: Writing creatively empowers students to interact with the world on their own, through their own experience and with their own language and perceptions. Writing in this way frees students—and us teachers, too—to see the power of their own voice, to feel silence ebb and voice emerge.

There is a beautiful passage from Paulo Freire's (1970) *Pedagogy of the Oppressed* that offers key insights into the notions of silence and voice, absence and presence:

> Human existence cannot be silent, nor can it be nourished by false words, but only by true words, with which men and women transform the world. To exist, humanly, is to *name* the world, to change it. Once named, the world in its turn reappears to the namers as a problem and requires of them a new *naming*. Human beings are not built in silence, but in word, in work, in action-reflection.
>
> But while to say the true word—which is work, which is praxis—is to transform the world, saying that word is not the privilege of some few persons, but the right of everyone. Consequently, no one can say a true word alone—nor can she say it *for* another, in a prescriptive act which robs others of their words. (p. 69; italics added)

How might students have been robbed of the process of naming the world? Freire states boldly that to exist as a human demands using one's voice—"Human existence cannot be silent." Therefore, the silences that students (and teachers!) experience in classrooms even as they speak and write and work on assignments (because silence is not simply *inaction;* it is also the presence of *unauthentic* action) can sometimes negate their most basic sense of humanity. Freire states that only true words can nourish this sense of humanity, or humanness, and that true words have the basic function of transforming the world. Students may see their world as belonging to the dominant class; perhaps the teacher has practiced subtle (or not so subtle) forms of assimilation, or perhaps classmates have been able to create a mirage of power and dominance. Or perhaps they're just so hepped up on an endless stream of YouTube clips and Hollywood movies that they gave up long ago on trying to think and name for themselves. Through creative writing, the process of seeing another world becomes entirely plausible and possible.

Freire's idea that only *after* naming the world does one actually *see* the world as a problem is fascinating. Before a student names the world, it seems fine; it appears as though it is the same as it has always been. The world, in other words, is not where the problem lies; instead, the problem lies with the student. It is she or he who must change; the world will remain stable and constant. However, in taking the leap to actually *name* the world, it becomes at once activated, fluid, and unpredictable. Anything can happen. Through language and action, the world now "reappears" as it really is: problematic. The world-as-problem presents the greatest possibility for students to succeed in that it takes as its highest aim *not* assimilation but rather *reflection* and *action*. We might make the small leap from here to state that *action* and *reflection* are merely synonyms for *creation* and *criticism* in the field of creative writing. Thus, in making the choice to explore, describe, and experience the world as it really is, students end up exploring, describing, and experiencing their own authentic selves, their own emotions and feelings, and the world as it really is. Narrative, story, and creative writing are a medium for precisely that work.

One final insight of Freire's from the passage above is crucial to contemplate here. Freire states that no true words can be claimed "alone" or through a "prescriptive act." The nature of *naming* and of speaking truth must be relational, and it must not be as an answer to a prescribed dilemma that is posed by a figure of authority (a prescriptive act). Instead, the ability to speak true and name authentically can exist only when a relationship of equality is present, where the speaker does not speak in order to arrive at a predecided correct location. The voice the speaker uses might often be unsure of where it is going, what truth it is pursuing, and what names it will give the world. Another way of considering Freire's claim, here, is to say that the process of naming is more important than the eventual name. *Naming* is an active, work-oriented activity for which there is no specific and prescribed outcome. That would "rob" others of their authentic words. Adrienne Rich (1986), in her critical essay "Blood, Bread, and Poetry," articulates the same idea as Freire like this: "Every group that lives under the naming and image-making power of a dominant culture is at risk from this mental fragmentation and needs an art which can resist it" (p. 244). Rich rephrases Freire's problem and claims that a possible solution is the use of an "art."

As English teachers, creative writing offers itself to us like a loaf of garlic bread, toasted perfectly so that the butter is completely melted, the garlic infused, and the squishiness factor precisely right. In other words, creative writing says, *I'm here! Use me! I'm that art!*

MORE TO THE MIX

Just because you're interested in empowering your students to use their authentic voices to interact with the world as it really is—the very act of creation—does not mean that writing rules, standards, and techniques should be any less rigorous. Indeed, the case can be made that creative writing is, in some ways, far more difficult than traditional analytical writing. When writing creatively, one cannot simply type, "The man felt sad." Well, one *could* type those words, but the truth is, they make for a lousy sentence. The reader who relishes a story or a poem or a novel or a play longs to know, *how* does the man feel sad? Does he feel sad like I felt sad when my cat of 17 years died? Or does he feel sad like I felt sad when I was a kid and was always picked last for the dodgeball game? How does his sad *look*? In other words, a reader wants to be compelled to believe, innately and without doubt, that the character is entirely flesh and bones and pumping organs and spaghetti brains—exactly like you and me. This is why, as you pursue creative writing with your students, you'll challenge them to get beyond "The man felt sad."

As a starting point, I hand out "Mr. Reynolds's List of Writing Rules" (Appendix M). I try to make the process of learning some rather difficult guidelines a fun and funny one by giving it my own tone and style. Just because there are guidelines to writing creatively, however, doesn't have to make the process any less joyful. I try not to deaden my students with requirements, especially at the start, when they are just learning to feel some confidence and freedom to create plots, characters, and worlds. For instance, it would be ghastly to read a student's first two novella pages and then refer them to my list and show them how they've failed numbers 3, 7, and 9. *No!* There's no more surefire way to turn our students off to writing than to tell them it doesn't measure up. Consider it from this perspective: As a teacher, when you taught your first lessons, you either had a helpful and encouraging chair and observer, or you had the opposite. Many a potentially good teacher has been turned off to the profession and rejected their calling because they had someone hell-bent on criticizing their every decision. Creative writing is more like growing flowers than it is like cutting down a forest to make a parking lot. We do our students a disservice by bulldozing their efforts in the name of "raising the bar" or anything like that when they need some hearty doses of water and sunshine.

Once students start to feel some confidence and joy in creating original work, however, it becomes time to mix in some weeding. A list like the one I give my students (Appendix M) gives me helpful guidelines as I revise student writing, have one-on-one conferences, and try to help their stories grow meaningful and vivid. Along these lines, using chapters from books like Lamott's (1995) *Bird by Bird* is incredibly encouraging because the tone in books on craft is a far cry from what students are used to in textbook descriptions of writing. For example, one chapter in Lamott's book is aptly titled "Shitty First Drafts," and I can honestly report that my 11th-graders would say reading that chapter aloud in class was one of the highlights of their year (and, okay, fine, I confess—it was a highlight of mine as well). Lamott gets at that core need we all know students hate, but in a fresh and inspired way. Instead of thinking of revision and editing as boring and dreadful, students see that even a professional, published, and award-winning writer feels that her fiction is awful when she begins crafting it. But she keeps at it. She revises. She rethinks. She re-creates. Students, when they see how writing actually functions in the world outside the walls of the classroom, will often rise to the occasion as well. (By the way, you've now heard mention of Lamott's book numerous times; so if you haven't read *Bird by Bird*, do so—it's essential reading for every English teacher and, I would humbly suggest, every human being.)

SHORT ASSIGNMENTS

If the idea of incorporating a novella or other long creative project into your curriculum sounds daunting or if you're starting to wonder if this Luke Reynolds guy is really *all there*, hold on! There are other ways of incorporating highly creative writing into your classroom that are simpler and more short term. Take, for example, the exercise "Writing Authentic Dialogue" (Appendix N). Writing authentic dialogue is very difficult even for most professional writers. Yet, as readers, when we reach long sections in novels or short stories that feel "true" or "real," we don't often stop reading and say, "Wow, that dialogue is really working!" Writing good dialogue is one of the skills that we only notice when it's not working. In the assignment, I ask my students to think about our class discussions and notes on *showing rather than telling* in writing, and I include a model of some dialogue that I attempted to make as authentic as possible. It's an actual conversation, and I tried to put it into words as best as I could. When I share my own creative writing with students, they can both see an imperfect model and feel my vulnerability as an educator and a writer. This encourages them to feel freer in their writing and shows that no writing is perfect the first time around—or even the third, or the thirty-third time around! Editing and honing our work as writers—and teachers—never comes to an end.

Another way to to include short creative assignments is by using prompts. The ones in "Brief, Personal Writing Prompts" (Appendix O) challenge students to write creatively about situations that feel real, and I ask them to respond to the prompts while writing from their own point of view or that of a character they have invented or have written about previously (in their novella, a short story, or a poem). Additionally, prompts like these can double as responses to literature if you invite students to respond creatively to one of the included prompts as, for example, Twain's Huck Finn might, or Salinger's Holden Caulfield, or Flake's Maleeka Madison. These brief prompts can be combined with a unit on the American Dream (as was the case when I made them) or with a unit on conflict, decision making, or fate (all frequent themes in many great novels and stories). Creative writing prompts can become an authentic learning tool if you craft prompts that include very real problems in the community.

An offshoot of the more traditional creative writing prompt is the use of narrative openings. Here, you might construct the start of a short story that employs a voice that is strong, character-driven, and intense. When you give this starter to your students, they are free to take the story any way they'd like to, and what results are 25 different versions all centered on the same dilemma. I use narrative openings to help my students learn point of view; for example, using the second-person narrative voice, made famous in Jay McInerney's (1984) *Bright Lights, Big City*, is not common for most students, and often they have never written in this POV or even read much that employs it. Additionally, narrative openings set the stage for excellent class discussions on perspective and analysis of one another's work. This type of writing also works well with poetry, where you might write the opening three lines of a poem and then instruct your students to finish the work. Also, using published material (such as a short story you will read as a class after the writing activity, or a poem you will explore) can some-times enhance the excitement students feel when they later read the same start to a story or poem they have written; they can then compare their own decisions as authors to the published author's choice. This, too, lends itself to excellent class discussions of *how* an author makes meaning and the criteria for what makes a story memorable, meaningful, and powerful.

Another way to utilize short creative writing assignments is through combining story with the need to teach other skills (such as grammar tools and vocabulary building). You might list five difficult vocabulary words on the board, ask students to find their definitions, and then have them write their own short stories (using a prompt you've created or entirely from their own ideas) in which they must include all of the vocabulary words. An extension of the way to use this idea and make it more challenging is to have students start their stories with no preselected words. Then, while writing, they must keep an eye on the whiteboard or chalkboard. Every few minutes, you place a new word on the board with its definition. The students have until the next word goes up to use the current word in their stories. You can also place literary terms on the board with a game like this—such as *metaphor, alliteration*, or *assonance*. The time component can be a fun addition, as long as students know it is a fun challenge and not meant to be a strict and graded enterprise.

THE RIDICULOUS AND FREE AS A BRIDGE TO PEARLS OF WISDOM: AN ASSIGNMENT IN FOCUS

One final suggestion for a short assignment is helpful here. It warrants a disclaimer, however, before I introduce the method. I am a believer in what many professional writers suggest about creativity—that in order to get to the pearls, we must often wade through the muck. In other words, when using creative writing in the class-room, we cannot expect our students or ourselves to pour forth beauty in a single class period or in a homework assignment. Instead, we would do our students a great service to help them see that allowing their minds to freely roam and write can produce pearls. These pearls can later be used to birth longer stories, poems, or other texts. We cannot consistently tell ourselves and our students, "No, that won't work. Nope—not that, either. That makes no sense! That is far too silly! Ah—no way. You can't write about a thing like that. Or that. OR THAT. And, no, definitely not that." These kinds of reactions shut down the creative process midstream. Many students have already experienced these kinds of voices for many years by the time they reach our classrooms.

In his powerful book *Writing Without Teachers*, Peter Elbow (1973) asserts that good writing often does not simply arrive, polished and perfect. He suggests that perhaps older notions of teaching writing through a series of hard-and-fast stages is not always the best route—for creative *or* critical work. Prewriting, brainstorming, graphic organizers, appropriate/inappropriate labels—all might possibly prevent good writing from ever actually being created. "It is simply a fact that most of the time you can't find the right words till you know exactly what you are saying, but that you can't know exactly what you are saying till you find just the right words. The consequence is that you must *start by writing the wrong meanings in the wrong words*; but keep writing till you get the right meanings in the right words" (p. 26). Elbow's expertise here suggests that removing all creativity from the writing process is neither good writing nor good teaching. In essence, sometimes good writing can occur only when bad writing has occurred first. In other words, an initial burst of creativity may prove more helpful in the long run than hours and hours of relentless critical thinking about writing. Writing, like a person, is generally complex, but it is far more fun and inspiring (and even more productive) to embrace that complexity and messiness than to demand cleanliness and categories all the time.

Before moving on to my final example of a short assignment, it's helpful to bolster this notion of writing as exploration—as creative endeavor—by returning to, you guessed it, Anne Lamott (1995). In the "Shitty First Drafts" chapter of *Bird by Bird*, discussed earlier, she writes: "The first draft is the child's draft, where you let it all pour out and then let it romp all over the place, knowing that no one is going to see it and that you can shape it later. You just let this childlike part of you channel whatever voices and visions come through and onto the page. . . . Just get it all down on paper, because there may be something great in those six crazy pages that you would never have gotten to by more rational, grown-up means" (p. 23). Lamott's claim suggests that the "more rational, grown-up means" are what all of us eventually learn are the proper ways of proceeding. However, are these "rational, grown-up means" really the only route to rigor of quality, merit, and intellectual growth and capability?

I often use an activity I simply call "Listening to Random Thoughts" (Appendix P) with my students. Essentially, I describe the creative process as one that is holistic, inclusive of everything that passes through our minds and hearts. As we search for story, meaning, words, and voices, we must learn to capture all that we think, see, experience, feel, and contemplate. The conscious mind is prone to reject ideas, so when we learn to write creatively, we reverse this habit. We try to strengthen the mind muscle that says, "I don't care if this is silly, ridiculous, or nonsensical. I am going to write it anyway and trust that it may yield the seeds of something profound, meaningful, and worthwhile. If I don't give these seemingly silly ideas and notions expression, I may never get to the really beautiful stuff that follows."

What I mean to say here is that creativity does not just happen. Someone *allows* it to happen, *encourages* it to happen, and then works to *make it* happen. I discuss the idea of a "random thought" with my students as we consider what it means to be creative. My view of a random thought is, simply, an inkling of an idea that flies quickly through the mind and then is gone forever. We have thousands of these thoughts every day. Few of us would give more than a passing nod (if that) at any of them. However, as students learn to find ideas for stories, poems, and plays of their own creation, this habit needs to change. Thus, one assignment I use with great effectiveness is the process of "Listening to Random Thoughts" (Appendix P). I give my students a block of time in class—perhaps 45 minutes or even an hour—and instruct them to record every single random thought that passes through their minds. No matter how silly, sensitive, weird, awkward, or sad it may be. Sometimes, if class time is short, an activity like this can be practiced at home, as an assignment. If this is the case, instruct students to sit uninterrupted for a block of time and simply write. They can use a computer or write longhand. Before I actually have students do this task—which, if built up enough, gets them quite excited—I share my own ramblings from a "Random Thoughts" session via the handout (Appendix P). We read through my sampling together, and they laugh at what I've done, but they also see the seeds of some lines or ideas that would be worth pursuing further. It may be that there is only one pearl amidst all of the gibberish, but there is one. And that pearl may be so beautiful that it becomes a story that would never have been born had we not given our over minds to the kind of creative freedom needed to forge something from nothing. Each time I have done this activity with students, they have been surprised at what they've written, and all have found pearls to which they returned for later writing assignments in class or in their own spare time.

CONCLUSIONS

Writing creatively in the middle and secondary classroom is an exercise in making something from nothing. Organic to that process is a bit of messiness, confusion, giddiness, fear, worry, and joy. These are all the things that professional writers experience, and by offering our students a taste of this process, we help them learn about writing in general while enabling them to possess a much greater understanding of the novels, stories, poems, and plays we explore in our literature courses. Indeed, one can spend all the time in the world analyzing a desk, a shelf, or a cabinet—discussing its purpose, flaws, and exquisite characteristics—but an even deeper analysis and understanding is possible when one learns woodworking. The analyst can then discover how certain boards are cut, shaped, and combined to create the eventual whole. No amount of writing *about* can access these same levels of thinking, but the process of actively creating helps students learn to do this innately when there is an open, encouraging and guided environment.

GUIDING QUESTIONS

1. Are there any activities from this chapter and their corresponding assignments in the Appendixes that interest you and that you would consider using?
2. What ideas about creativity interest you most, and what excites you about allowing your students to be more creative?
3. What scares you about seeing what your students might produce given this kind of prodding? What scares you about what *you* might produce?
4. Can you afford an hour of your time right now—or tonight, after the kids are asleep or once the grading is done—to try the "Random Thoughts" activity for yourself? Can you find an hour this weekend to try it? Can you think of a café nearby where you can go, with a cup of coffee in hand, and set to writing your hour's worth of silly, serious, and sad musings?
5. Make a list of your favorite novels, stories, or poems. No specific number is required. List them out on a blank page, and spend a bit of time thinking about each one, just remembering and relishing how much the words within moved you.
6. Say the following out loud: "No writer ever wrote anything meaningful without a little (or big) mess along the way."
7. Give yourself and your students permission to be a little (just a little to start!) messy and silly and goofy and free with their words, and trust that the creative process that has worked for centuries will take hold in your heart and theirs, as well!

CHAPTER 4

Doing Outside the Box

Newton's first law of physics states that an object in motion will remain in motion (at the same uniform rate) unless it is acted upon by an external force. The corollary to this law is that an object at rest will remain at rest unless acted upon by an external force. Consider our students. Some of their lives are deeply in motion along arcs that seem to be headed in ways that are unhealthy and dangerous or that do not utilize their full potential. Other students may appear to be deeply at rest. Thus, as an English teacher, *you* can sometimes be that external force so precisely described by Newton. But sometimes it becomes difficult (or even impossible) to find the energy to uniquely affect each student and get his or her trajectory headed in a more passionate, purposeful way. This is where it's vital to get students outside the walls of your classroom and outside the walls of the school.

CREATIVITY BEYOND THE CLASSROOM

After teaching at the secondary level for a while, I assigned my 11th-grade students a fairly open-ended essay on the theme of love. Part of my motivation was the recent experience of classroom dialogues that were incredibly moving and also quite funny. The assignment was simple: two pages on love—your experiences with it, reflections on it, its possibility or not, and anything else you deem worthwhile to include. There was purposely very little structure.

When the reflections came in, I stayed late after school and sat in my empty classroom reading them. All 50 of them. I simply couldn't stop reading. Usually, when I read student work, it's a constant battle for me to keep my pen off the page for more than a few seconds. I am a great fan of marginalia, and I annotate like crazy on student pages (though using a calmer blue ink rather than the eerie, traditional red). This time, however, my hand was steady under my chin as I read, and read, and read. I laughed out loud, I cried, and I smirked, smiled, and nodded. My students had written honestly about love—as honestly as they could, and it brought a whole heap of joy to my heart.

Later that night, as I lay in bed tossing and turning, I could not stop thinking about those love essays. I am sure that my wife, Jennifer, also endured a miserable night due to my inability to stop thinking about my students' writing on love, and even our new cat, Lewis, was annoyed.

In the days to come, I considered my own dreams of publishing a book. I had received many rejection letters already for my writing—one of which came from an editor aptly named William Slaughter—but I thought that maybe this was an opportunity to combine my passions for teaching and writing, to use some of the knowledge I had gained about publishing through my journey of rejection. So I broached the topic with my two 11th-grade classes: Would you be interested in trying to form an anthology of all your writing on love, editing and honing your words and ideas, and seeing if there's a publisher out there who'd be interested in helping the book meet some readers in the world?

Their response: HECK YEAH!

Prior to this moment, I had talked at length about social justice issues in our classroom. We had read and viewed much in the wake of Hurricane Katrina, and we discussed the underlying implications of poverty, looked at the causes of a highly unequal distribution of wealth in America and all over the world, and examined gender inequality (with the help of a remarkable documentary entitled *Tough Guise* [Jhally, 1999], produced by the Media Education Foundation and narrated by anti-violence educator Jackson Katz). So, when I introduced the idea of the anthology, I asked my students how they would feel about donating any money a book like this might make to an organization that works toward social justice. All were on board, and we set off on a roller coaster of a ride.

We spent about a month revising their essays, mostly before and after school, trying out different titles, collating the manuscript, considering order, and formatting the manuscript. Then I set to work using what I had learned about the publishing industry. I e-mailed a slew of agents, knowing that—for the most part—before a book can sell, an agent is necessary to get it into the hands of editors at a publishing house. Almost all of the agents I queried expressed no interest. But three said they'd like to see the material. So I packed up two envelopes with our class manuscript and e-mailed one attachment. A month later, I read the three rejections out loud to my class. I was beginning to see that this was also a teachable moment about what an author goes through *before* a book ever sees the light of day. However, I'd be lying if I said that I didn't feel sad to see their heartbroken faces.

The process of submitting our manuscript to agents and, eventually, to small publishers and presses continued for a few months. I started to think that it wasn't going to happen, and I wondered if I even should have broached this with my students—*Why get them excited about a possibility that would, very likely, end in failure?* When I thought about shelving the manuscript—as I did with my own writing when it had garnered enough rejections from the likes of William Slaughter—it was my wife, Jennifer, who said to give it another try. (Author note: Jennifer is some kind of miracle worker, always insisting that I give it another try no matter what *it* is; probably 90% of my hare-brained schemes in teaching, writing, living, and dreaming have become realities only because of her words.) My father, Harry, had suggested a small publisher called Stonegarden Publishing in California. So I sent the manuscript off as an attachment, and the reply came back that Kristofer Stamp, the publisher, wanted to make our little idea into a book. When the book was released a year later, entitled *Inside Out and Outside In: Essays on the Nature and Experience of Love* (Reynolds, 2007), it was a beautiful little thing.

We had decided, as a class, that the proceeds from the book would benefit Habitat for Humanity, a remarkable organization that helps build homes for those in need by enlisting the aid of community members and donations of materials. While our book certainly broke no records and made no big sales, it did raise some money for Habitat, and it did show my students that their abilities as writers and creators could have a life outside of our classroom. This trial run taught me a lot about the publishing process, and I sensed that a Round #2 might be in store in the future . . .

MAKING THE CLASSROOM ANTHOLOGY MANAGEABLE, CHEAP, AND EFFECTIVE

Years later, I still swear by the classroom anthology. It's an essential part of any literature or writing class. Consider the raw material and imagination at your fingertips: 20 or more students. Paper. Pencils. Computers. Examples of loads of books. A world full of worthy causes. So many battles to fight.

When we add up all of these materials, we may seek to go where teacher and writer Frederick Buechner exhorted, to the place "where your deep gladness and the world's deep hunger meet" (p. 95, 1973/1993). Indeed, for any teacher who loves literature and writing, using a classroom anthology as a way to respond to one of the world's greatest needs is an inspiring way to live out Buechner's line.

In my 7th-grade class, we read *The Breadwinner* by Deborah Ellis (2004). It is a powerful fictional account of a young girl in Afghanistan, growing up under the rule of the Taliban. It shocked my students to see the way women are treated—men as well—under this brutal and oppressive power. After reading the book, we researched Women for Women International, the organization to which Ellis donates all of her royalties from that volume. We also viewed a powerful documentary on women in Afghanistan. My students, of their own accord, began to ask if we could help out Women for Women International. I smiled and replied, "I know just the way we can."

Months later, my 7th-graders and I had a complete book. This time around, we used a local printer to produce 200 copies of the book. My students were aglow when the boxes were delivered to our classroom, and together we spent a full period rereading our own words—and anticipating our upcoming time at the local grocery store on Saturday.

It remains one of the most beautiful sights I have ever witnessed as a teacher: 7th-grade jocks mixing with 7th-grade computer whizzes mixing with 7th-grade drama queens mixing with 7th-grade silent-types. A horde of students gathered like a battalion of soldiers at the entrance to the local Stop & Shop. We priced each book at five dollars, and students ran up to customers merely looking to buy a gallon of milk who, instead, got an earful about an anthology whose proceeds would benefit Women for Women International.

When all was said and done, we had raised almost $500. The next week, in school, I asked our secretary to make a cashier's check out to Women for Women, and I forked over the dough. It was a beautiful thing to show that check to my students and to be able to say in all honesty, "The writing that *you* all created is going to help feed, free, and teach women in countries where they are oppressed, just as we learned about in *The Breadwinner*." I saw pride and excitement written on every one of their faces. They left class feeling good about their own work and how it had moved outside the classroom to make a difference—albeit a small one—in the world beyond the school walls.

So how can you help your classes create an anthology and use it to generate funds so that it becomes an exercise in writing skills, entrepreneurial techniques, interaction beyond the classroom walls, and social justice? Let's briefly break down the process.

First, it is important to understand that as a teacher you will need to lead the process, but the engine behind it must be your students. Your own excitement will ignite theirs. But don't think that the responsibility is yours alone for proofreading, collating, organizing, making phone calls, and selling and distributing.

Second, try to provide an outline of the project to your students at its inception so that they know all the steps involved and can feel empowered to bring it to fruition.

Third, decide how you want the essays to be crafted: Will you choose the theme for the entire book (as I did for my first anthology with my 11th-graders, on love)? Or will you allow your students to select themes and divide the anthology into multiple parts (as I did with later anthologies)? Create an assignment—much like you would create any assignment that involves the required parts of an essay—and engage your students with the task. *Be excited!* Remind them (constantly, to the point where they become severely annoyed with you) that this book will be read by people from all over your town—-maybe even by people from other towns! It helps to dream with students—and you might encourage students who don't necessarily love writing to get more involved by using their other talents: Maybe they can design a website that showcases the book; maybe they can create cover or internal artwork; maybe they are great social networkers and can use Facebook to get some buzz going. In other words, this is an ideal project through which to get your students excited about using what they know to get writing outside the classroom and also make a difference in the world.

Fourth, rigorously revise the writing students hand in—but don't do it alone. If you try to make every student essay as good as it can be, you'll lose all your marbles and maybe even go into marble-debt. Instead, create other ways to revise: Use peer-editing methods; host after-school editorial board sessions (where students lead revisions rather than you); ask education/English majors at local colleges if they'd like to be involved (for them, it looks great on their résumé, it gives them hands-on editing experience and book experience, and you can promise them you'll thank them in the Acknowledgments section of your book); and even recruit your own mom or dad or another retired teacher. In other words, *involve other people*. For one of our anthologies, a kind class mother brought my editorial board hot chocolate and doughnuts, and I can report wholeheartedly that it was our best editing session of all.

Fifth, delegate some students (four or five) to be in charge of collating the entire book. It will be their responsibility to, essentially, use a shared flash drive or open e-mail attachments (however you choose to electronically get all student essays submitted to you) and paste each student essay into a master document. Once this step is accomplished, you essentially have the rough draft of a book. And, if you're anything like me, it's a thrilling feeling to look down to the left on your computer screen when that document is open and see the page number read: 205.

Sixth, since you now have the rough draft of an anthology, with each essay in good shape, having been revised by multiple other students, college kids, retired teachers, the secretary (I'm serious—sometimes they really want to be involved—why not ask?), the janitor (again: yes, I'm serious), the principal (why not—she or he can take time to revise two or three essays, right?), and anyone else you can enlist to help the cause, you're ready to write and insert your own Introduction. As a teacher, this is your chance to speak to the community, and at a time like this, it's a *great* chance to describe why writing matters, why passion for words matters, and why teaching and interacting with students is such a sacred opportunity. My Introductions for my class anthologies are usually fairly brief—around 500 or 600 words—but I like to stress how hard my students worked, how much writing matters to us all, and the importance of social justice and making a difference in the world. (See "Introduction to Anthology Project," Appendix Q, for a model; it's an Introduction I wrote for one of my 7th-grade class anthologies.) Creating a book like this also allows the community to see what your students create.

Seventh, read through the book and proofread it for basic errors. Try not to make too many changes at this point, but catch any typos that always, *always* seem to occur—like dust that gathers in corners only minutes after vacuuming! You can again enlist one or two additional readers at this point if you like. While you're reading through the manuscript, delegate to students the responsibility of phoning some printers or even copy centers like Staples and Kinko's to get price quotes for the number of copies you will print or copy at the current (approximate) page length. If it's your first anthology, you may want to shoot for around 200 copies. I always give one away to each student for free, and some parents always want to buy ten copies (to give to every single relative and neighborhood dog and cat)—and this is a great way to get the book out there and create funds for your cause! (It is important to note, by the way, that up to this point you have spent absolutely no money and—even though my explanation of the steps has been long—you haven't depleted yourself doing massive amounts of work. Meanwhile, you have given your students an incredible experience that reaches outside the walls of the classroom, connects to the community, and helps a good cause in our world.)

Eighth, as a class, decide on things like the cover image, color, and what will appear on the back of the book (information about the cause the sales will benefit?

graphics? background on your class?). I use the simple democratic process to make these decisions with my classes, and this can also be a lesson in a host of other things (governmental procedure, community decision making, marketing, sales, etc.). Once your class has decided, enlist a handful of students to work with you as you scan the front and back cover images, type the text, create a Table of Contents, and check over everything one last time.

Ninth is beautiful. Simply stunning. It's where you e-mail or bring a CD or flashdrive of your manuscript to the printer/copy center. The turnaround time is usually quite fast, so you and your students can whisper together in the hallways, "Is it here yet?" and, "Oh, it's going to be thrilling when it gets here!" You'll find that even students who seemed distant and apathetic begin to care about seeing what it's going to look like when all is said and done. After all, *their* words are going out into the world. Okay, just a tiny part of the world—but still: People other than *you*, their teacher, are going to read what they've written. This is a truly gigantic event.

Tenth, ask the janitor to help you get four or five heavy cardboard boxes out of the trunk of your car and into your classroom at 6 o'clock in the morning. You stand in your classroom alone for a while, open up one of the boxes, flip through the contents of the *book* you and your students have created, and think about Habitat for Humanity, or Women for Women International, or Free the Slaves, or the Children's Defense Fund, or whichever cause you've decided to support. You smile. When each class comes in, you tell them how proud of them you are; you say they've become *authors*, not just writers, now; and you give them their free copy of the book. You allow them a full period to read over it and be excited. And then, before the bell rings, you remind them that the first part is over, and it sure was exciting. Now it's time to sell. You implement your marketing plan—whether it's simply to sell to parents and grocery stores, along with some door-to-door, as it was with my later class anthologies, or whether it's to have a student create a website and sell using a PayPal button, or something else.

It may sound like a lot, but a project like this can actually be much more pain-free than it seems. One major benefit of using the classroom anthology in a literature course is that it enables students to see what being an author is really like: It invites them into a rigorous revision process aimed at an audience that extends beyond you and your red (or blue) pen. Additionally, it opens students' eyes to organizations that seek to heal the hurting in our world—the kind of hurting that is often the subject of our greatest literature, whether in Deborah Ellis's (2004) *The Breadwinner* or Elie Wiesel's (1960/2006) *Night*. There are enough connections to literature, writing, and every standard imaginable to make one's mind explode with glee. (If you still feel confused, worried, anxious, or incredulous, e-mail me at LWReynolds@gmail.com for further thoughts, encouragements, ideas; to tell me I'm crazy; or to explain why this won't work in your classroom. However, be prepared for an array of incredibly hopeful, *you-can-do-it-isms* to come back at you.)

SMALL WAYS TO MAKE BIG CONNECTIONS OUTSIDE THE WALLS

In this section, I want to share one more brief way you might help your students make English *stuff* an activity that happens *outside* the walls of the classroom. It's something I do at the very end of every year, no matter which grade level I'm teaching. I call it the Book Awards. Essentially, it's a full class period of me telling each student that I know them, care for them, and hope they will become lifelong readers and writers.

Specifically, I buy a book for each student prior to the Book Awards class period and write a note at the front of the book (as you would if giving the book to your daughter, son, husband, wife, or favorite aunt from Tennessee who makes the meanest banana-corn muffins around). I have the books all ready to go at the start of the class, and I have already prepped the students to be aware that I will severely embarrass them, stating their wonderful qualities aloud, and then making them come up to the front of the room to shake my hand as I give them their award: a book. It feels like a sports banquet. For reading.

If you're thinking, "This man is crazy," let me put your mind at ease a bit. Almost every town in every state in America has library book fairs. They are advertised all over town, on bulletin boards, and also online (do a search now for your area, and I guarantee that one will be coming up, somewhere within a radius of 10 miles of where you live, within the next month). These library book fairs are basically like a candy store for an English teacher: beautiful, amazingly good books for little money—often as low as 50 cents each! If you have 120 students, that's only 60 bucks to pick out a specific book for each kid. And you know, of course (as I recently learned by using Turbo Tax this year), that teacher expenses are tax-deductible. (Score!) Yes, you're spending some cash, but you'll get it back on your next year's tax return. Plus, the way your students will light up when you flatter them as they come up to receive their very own book that you have handpicked for them is, well, it's beyond words. It's what you live for as a teacher. And many students will actually *read* these books. They'll remember these gifts and reread what you wrote inside the covers for years to come. It's a small thing, but it ends up being a huge thing for your students. It reminds them that school is not something that just exists inside four walls. It helps them believe that reading, writing, and passion are always inseparable. And it shows them that, no matter what kind of crap they may have dished your way during the course of the year, you see their strengths and you hope they will be lifelong readers and lovers of the power of words.

CONCLUSIONS

I have been told that when I get into a giddy place, it is impossible to calm me down or help me be rational and cautious. Therefore, I add the following disclaimer: Thinking about classroom anthologies, Book Awards, and, generally, expanding the impact of the English classroom beyond the classroom walls gets me incredibly giddy. So consider yourself warned, and now we can proceed to a highly giddy conclusion.

Your heart longs to make teaching a crossroads of your life, where your own passion for and love of words, messages, and meanings have real impacts on the way you see the world around you and live your life. Our students have this very same desire. It's innate. Our students may have become quite adept at hiding it (and, indeed, we may have as well, if we've allowed certain standards or public opinion polls or documentaries to quench the fire in us). But we both know that the truth stands: We crave meaning. We want what we read to matter and make a difference. We want students to see how the words they read and the words they write can be more than answers to a test, fillers for a blank sheet, or a path to college and a high-paying job. In short, we want to feel, and we want our students to feel, alive. Using a classroom anthology or a tradition like the Book Awards can help this endeavor.

Perhaps you've read this chapter, and your heart and mind are nodding in agreement. Or perhaps by now you're thinking, "Man! How much did I spend on this book? I wonder if it's too worn to return to the bookstore and get my cash back?" In either case, I want to encourage you to ponder whether using one of these possibilities could work in your classroom, and, if not, to try creating something that could. Instead of beginning with the standard or the expectation that has been, extrinsically, put upon you, begin with the intrinsic and ask yourself: *How would I want to take my classroom beyond the walls?* As we discussed with the random thoughts lesson from the last chapter, as you think about this question, allow your mind to be truly free. Don't shoot down your own ideas, and don't let the voices of crushing criticism stop you before you get to the pearls of how *you* will get outside the walls.

Because you will. I know it.

GUIDING QUESTIONS

1. What excites or scares you about the idea of creating a classroom anthology?
2. What kinds of personal writing have you done? Have you ever dreamed about being a published author? Could you wake up some of that dream and translate it into a project with your students?
3. What kinds of connections do you have? Could you enlist the aid of others to help with class projects, or even to be involved in mentoring or guest speaking?
4. Consider your own life as a student. In what ways would you have *loved* to take writing and reading outside the classroom and into the real world? Make a list of what you loved most about your favorite English classes growing up.
5. Could you join forces with another colleague and do an anthology or another big project together?
6. Repeat the following line out loud three times: *My students will forget much of what I have them memorize, but every experience I invite them into will be burned into their minds forever!*

CHAPTER 5

Beyond Reading and Writing: How to Teach Students to See, Think, and Feel

WE'VE DISCUSSED a lot of practical ways to make creativity a relevant, inspiring, and intricate part of your teaching and your curriculum. However, it's also important to teach students (and ourselves) how to *think* and *see* in creative ways. Wayne Booth (1988), in the introduction to his powerful volume, *The Company We Keep*, makes this significant (but often ignored) claim: "Many critics today still resist any effort to tie 'art' to 'life,' the 'aesthetic' to the 'practical'" (p. 5). As we teach our students to creatively critique their own perspectives, consider new perspectives, and use literature as a lens to transform their own lives, we indeed do what Booth suggests: We tie art to life and we connect the aesthetic to the practical. I believe that this happens in the classroom through three powerful faculties: compassion, imagination, and trust through experience. Let's explore each component of making creativity a way of being and seeing rather than just something we try to *add* or *do* with our students.

COMPASSION

In her essay included in the book *Compassion*, Kathleen Woodward (2004) explores how the term has been muddied by years of political squabbling and chronicles its abuse by a variety of people and groups. As Woodward explores the true significance of compassion in her own mind, she uses a variety of literature to assert that what it does best is to provide a means by which the one who truly feels compassion is *transformed* and can never again return to old ways of thinking, perceiving, and acting. (How we might wish that for our students and ourselves! To be truly changed! Yes!)

In her profound discussion, Woodward claims that compassion can be reclaimed as an entity that has meaning and power when we view it as a bridge that leads to a variety of things: "social justice" (p. 67), "a multicultural education [and understanding]" (p. 67), "[*not*] the feeling . . . an end in itself" (p. 70), "justice" (p. 81), and, ultimately, "trust" (p. 82). She argues against embracing compassion only as a form of sentimentalism, by which I or you can say, "I feel so bad about this or that," and then move on with our lives. Instead, compassion can become the way in which I enter into a totally new vision of who I am in the context of who others are, and then allow that transformation to inform the way I think and act in society. Therefore, compassion can be one way through which students learn to see others for who they are and get beyond egocentric views of school and self that are relentlessly promulgated to them by the media. *But how? How can we help students feel compassion?* The first step is to examine ourselves as teachers and to ask how literature has inspired and ignited compassion inside of us.

For me, this transformation through compassion occurred as I read Fyodor Dostoevsky's *The Brothers Karamazov* (1880/2004). Though it has become cliché to say, "I saw myself in that story," it's true! The text also, however, showed me what I was not, and then, ultimately, led to a slight conversion of who I am.

In the character of Alyosha, I found a young man not unlike myself: He seeks faith yet also doubts the faith that he seeks; he finds himself the peacemaker (to use a modern term from American culture) within a family that seems to be falling apart; he finds worth through his connections with children, and eventually, he decides that he will spend his life teaching them and therefore stake out his own humanity in a world that feels corrupted and cruel. This decision to be a teacher of the young enables him to maintain his faith in God and in the larger purpose of the Russia where he lives.

While I could work to establish the connection I felt as a reader to Alyosha, I think it is a much more worthwhile endeavor to consider the ways in which his character transformed me—the way in which his example allowed me to feel compassion for his life and for the students whose lives I connect with as they feel their own pain, confusion, fear, and hope.

Alyosha helped to crystallize what I began to feel: my own ineptitude to "save" students from their suffering—abusive parents, fears, betrayal of friends, suicidal thoughts, perfectionism. Instead, I experienced glimpses in which I was able to love and care for my students *through* their suffering and confusion and fears and hopes. Without my reading of Alyosha, I doubt how clearly I would have experienced this conversion. Further, with Woodward's grounding comments in my own understanding of the life of compassion, I doubt I would have sought so fervently to dissociate myself from sentimental interpretations that lead to no worthwhile action, no inner conversions.

My experience of students in the classroom and of novels like *The Brothers Karamazov* shows me that an ethical inquiry of literature and of life stands on solid ground, and if I am willing to engage in it further, it *does* have the power to impact my own life and those of others through me. With Alyosha, I have come to believe that the impossible can, indeed, be done.

As we seek to translate this kind of conversion and connection to text through *compassion* for our students, the most effective way it can happen is by modeling. We hear this all the time as educators—how important it is to model our expectations, to model our assessments, to model everything we want our students to be able to do. Therefore, it is no leap to recognize that we must model how we want our students to see, feel, and think *compassionately*. So ask yourself: Which texts have called you out of your own skin and helped you recognize truth in another perspective? Which texts have challenged you to see the world in bigger ways or in different ways? How, in your own life, have you tied art to life? How have words moved you and changed you? What have you done to transform your compassion for characters and for people into action? And the most important question of all: Have you shared these things with your students?

Often, we fall into the trap of thinking that as teachers we must hide ourselves from our students. Parker Palmer (1998) argues beautifully that it is only by sharing who we really are that students can engage with us in authentic learning. If we hope for our creative projects, assessments, and avenues to yield fruit, then we must leap into the field of compassion, demonstrating for our students how it works in our own lives by helping us connect to characters and people.

IMAGINATION

Imagination's role in learning has been documented for years in scholarly journals and research projects. In her article in *Science* magazine, Mary Ellen Avery (2004) notes that the most significant modern discoveries have been made because of the scientist's ability to think beyond what is logical, possible, and proven. The very nature of scientific hypothesis, she says, is founded upon the fact that "the entire enterprise [scientific method] must start with imagination." She continues to write that "all of these approaches to solving human problems began with 'imagining something different'" (p. 571). Thinking beyond what we can directly see in front of us is a skill that the world's children have mastered, a standard to which *no child is left behind* simply because they are born with the innate ability to imagine.

Sora Song (2005), in an article in *Time*, conveys the findings of a fascinating study on make-believe in the lives of children, especially the influence of imaginary friends on a child. In the study, conducted by Marjorie Taylor of the University of Oregon and Stephanie Carlson of the University of Washington, the role of imagining in the life of a child is examined for its influence in their social and mental capacities. The study found that 65% of children through age 7 had at least one imaginary friend and that the presence of such a friend correlated with better verbal skills and a heightened ability to understand other points of view. The presence of such powers of imagination generally lead to children who "may have above-average IQs, be more creative, and smile and laugh more on the playground than other kids" (p. 2). Is it any wonder, then, that as more and more children are being forced to grow up faster, play outside less with their friends, memorize terms and test answers earlier and earlier, and take statewide, nationwide performance tests, the amount of childhood medication for depression and the claim that children are bored increase exponentially? The role of imagination in the playing lives of kids seems as preventative of social ills and problems as the best medicines.

Julius Lester (2000) writes a powerful account of the moral and social capacity of the imagination via literature in his article "Re-imagining the Possibilities":

> Literature invites us into realms of the soul by asking us to imagine that we are someone other than who we are. Literature requires that we temporarily put our egos in a box by the door and take on the spirit of others. Literature is the place where the possibility of blacks and whites and men and women experiencing each other is created. I am convinced that if I can bring you into my being through the use of the imagination, then I have created the possibility that you and I are more alike than we may have thought. (p. 289)

Have you ever wondered why children so love stories? I have yet to meet a young child who, when I ask if he would like me to tell him a very scary but very amazing story, says *no*. As a camp counselor for 5 years, a wilderness expedition leader for 4, and a teacher for 7, I have yet to come across a child whose eyes do not light up when I say these magic words: "Hey, I've got a really cool story for you."

As teachers, we encounter many students who tell us they think literature is boring and writing is just really hard or not enjoyable. They say poetry doesn't mean much to them and that they have not enjoyed reading since they were little kids. Is it an odd coincidence that many of the students I have taught, and those whom my colleagues discuss with me, say that reading and writing are not experiences they relish? Furthermore, is it also a coincidence that all 5-year-olds I have ever met tell me that they love reading and could make up a story on the spot about anything? My students come alive—their bodies leaning in—when I tell them that I have a story I want to tell them. They know that I am going to share some zany experience of my own life—about how my wife and I bought 100 cans of Progresso extra chunky soup because they were on sale or about an accident I was in that, according to the doctor, should have killed me. My own connections to literature help them see where theirs may lie, through the faculty of, yes, imagination. Their sense of the wonder of life is still very much alive. They want to hear stories, but they want to hear stories that truly carry them outside the uncaring walls of a factory-like high school. They want to, as Lester writes, experience the essence of *otherness*—of stepping into the life of another and living out that way of being.

Often, this capacity for imagination is destroyed by those of us who would use high-stakes testing and relentless data-driven conclusions as methods of educational salvation. Instead, some of the solution to our turmoil in schools lies in the defunct status of our imagination, both individually and collectively. If we can help our students retain a sense of wonder, curiosity, and thrill about life—a sense of thirst for stories and for the imagination—then we can feel more alive *and be more productive* as a society. If we aren't willing to encourage the imaginations of our students, then we run the risk of losing what Jim Burke (2009) calls *real ideas*—ideas that actually grow, change, and improve the world in which we live. Burke writes powerfully in a splendid issue of *The English Journal* on imagination that "scores on tests do not translate into creativity or imagination; nor do such tests and the curriculum that prepares students to take them allow for the messy, fuzzy, risky thinking that leads to real ideas" (p. 12). When we as teachers encourage imagination in our students, the result is not only changed classrooms and transformed schools, but also a new and better world. As Burke so eloquently shares:

> It is, it seems, truly a brave new world unfolding around and before us. Moreover, it is one we are called to help our students not only understand but also to create, for theirs is the largest generation in the history of the world, one that will need all these roles if they are to enjoy the success they so easily imagine will inevitably be theirs. And it will be, theirs and ours, if we can make room for such imagination, creativity, and innovation as today's classrooms need if tomorrow's students are to succeed. (p. 14)

Indeed, instead of ruining the chances for student work and learning to yield real results in the world, empowering students to use their imaginations in our classrooms actually enhances what they will one day be able to accomplish. (That, and it makes learning a whole heck of a lot more fun.)

TRUST THROUGH EXPERIENCE

Okay, has Reynolds really gone and completely lost it now? This is, after all, a book about creativity in an age of standardization. What, therefore, does a touchy-feely word like *trust* have to do with anything?

It has everything to do with everything. Have you ever been in a group—maybe eating lunch somewhere, or sitting in a professional meeting, or even among a circle of friends or acquaintances—and felt undeniably, unspeakably *awkward*? Just incredibly out of place and somewhat scared to say what you really think or act like the person you really are? If you are among the 99.99% of us who are quite human and vulnerable and, well, sometimes insecure, then you've felt this kind of worry or discomfort. The important question is: *Why?* It's not necessarily that the people in the group were calling you names like *butt-face* and pointing at you and laughing. (If they were, I would seriously urge you to find new friends and groups in which to socialize!) Rather, it's because we didn't feel a sense of belonging, freedom, or . . . yup: *trust*. We were afraid to speak our words because we didn't trust that the people we were with would receive them. We were worried about how these people perceived us because we didn't think they cared enough to *really* see us. We all know this emotion, and, essentially, it feels like utter crap.

Students know this feeling all too well. Many students feel as though their peers, teachers, administrators, and parents are unwilling to really *see* them for who they are—faults and successes and everything in between. When we encourage creativity in our students' work and in their lives, we also encourage trust. When we challenge students to create meaningful writing that matters to them *and* us, the message between the lines is really: I *care* what you think, how you think, and why you think that, and I want to know what makes your heart beat fast. In other words, we are telling our students that it's okay for them to trust us and, in turn, to trust themselves, too.

One way I try to create a classroom built on trust may make you laugh. But then again, we're not sitting at the same table right now, so if you laugh and point your finger at me and call me *butt-face*, well, I can't see you. I use the activities described in detail in "Community-Forming Activities" (Appendix R). I acknowledge that many of them seem corny and naïve. However, I have used these activities (gleaned from my time as a wilderness guide) with high-income, low-income, "gifted," and "alternative" classes, and they have always been effective. Doing some of these experiential activities is a powerful hands-on experience for students and helps them actually envision the kind of trust I speak about with them. I preface any of these activities with a lot of serious talk about trust and vulnerability, and it helps to remind students that if you as a teacher or they as students are unwilling to be vulnerable with and trust one another, very little authentic learning, growth, or *real* enjoyment is going to happen.

I also try to model trust in the way I interact with students, the way I conference with them for revisions on an essay, the way I look them in the eyes when they speak and when I speak to them, and the way I try to be as honest as possible (even when it hurts, like admitting that I'm clueless about the very good question they've posed, or that I am actually blanking on the year Shakespeare was born, or that I, too, feel inexplicably exhausted sometimes).

One way I try to build trust and prepare students for a creative classroom experience is through teaching the art of conversation—and the importance of eye contact. What does conversing have to do with creativity? If being creative is a uniquely necessary component of what it means to be human—as this book takes as its premise—than conversing is an equally essential component of preparing to be creative in a trusting environment. In other words, when we embody the notion of *voicefulness*—or using our voices as a preliminary step toward creative expression—we are most ready to creatively share our stories, our ideas, our lives.

I learned that conversation is sacred when I was a 13-year-old kid in 8th grade, without a clue of who I was—confused, scared, and ready to copy anything my peers suggested. Into this malaise came my older brother, Christopher. As a deaf adolescent, Chris had endured more than his share of ridicule and bullying from classmates as he passed through the grades of the public school system in a suburb of Hartford, Connecticut. Growing up, Chris and I were not especially close, but by the time I was finishing 8th grade and Chris was preparing for his sophomore year at the University of Connecticut, our relationship had transformed into an especially close one.

Through Chris, I learned to communicate. Whereas I had been used to looking at my feet when I spoke with other people—or glancing around in a distracted and distractible manner—Chris's deafness denied me that ambivalence in conversation. Once the two of us began going out for a meal, running together, or talking when he came home for a visit from college, he taught me to look him straight in the eyes. It was the only way for Chris to be able to read my lips and comprehend what I was saying. Whenever I forgot this essential component of speaking with Chris, he would grab my chin and tilt my face toward him so that my eyes met his and he could follow the words I uttered. This gesture was especially poignant when it forced me to realize how often I stared at the ground as I spoke, rather than confidently meeting the gaze of whomever I was talking with.

To extrapolate from my experience with Chris into my life from that point forward, I began to look for the eyes of every person with whom I spoke. Because of Chris, I began to see how frequently others did not look me full in the face—and at a fairly young age I began asking: *Why not?*

I use one full class period to practice this forgotten form of communication. Before my students enter the classroom, I place all of the chairs into sets of two, facing each other. These sets of chairs are scattered all around with a substantial open space in the center of the classroom. As the students gather inside the room, they come to the center—excitedly questioning what this room rearrangement is meant to achieve. I begin this activity by sharing my own personal journey of my brotherhood with Chris, and the students are consistently engaged by his deafness, wondering what his life has been like, why people made fun of him in school, and what he is doing now. After sharing about the way that Chris taught me to communicate, I explain the activity. Students will be placed in pairs, and we will begin a series of conversations. At first I do not tell them how long they'll talk, but I ask them to sit across from each other and chat about anything—the only stipulation being that they cannot stop talking. *And they cannot look away from each other.* As students awkwardly begin talking (often with incredibly anxious and embarrassed grins), I walk around the room and poke them whenever they look away from their partner. It keeps the activity fun, but it reminds them that I'm *very* serious about them looking their partners in the eyes. After 5 minutes, I tell them they can stop talking.

We then gather our chairs into a circle, and I use a lot of the debriefing questions included at the end of Appendix R. Students are usually *shocked* that they have only spent 5 minutes talking with their partners. They say that it felt like 10 or 15 minutes. They share how awkward they felt, and they notice how often they *wanted* to look away. The activity begins to teach them that trust is possible if we, as a classroom community, can begin to start really seeing one another. An activity like this is aided by repetition in other forms, and I consistently encourage my students to make eye contact in every kind of classroom experience.

GETTING (PHYSICALLY) OUTSIDE THE SCHOOL AND INTO THE WORLD'S CLASSROOM

One irreplaceable way that trust through experience can be forged is by taking your students on field trips. I know that many teachers and districts are limited by funding, red tape, and an endless array of paperwork requirements, but if you can find a way through all of that (by being creative yourself—raising funds creatively and coming up with creative proposals and reasons why this trip is a *must* for you and your classes), then the journey to a special place is worth many days of classroom activities and lectures. When you share experiences with your students, you show yourself to be trustworthy to them, and you help them learn to trust one another and what their eyes perceive in new and exciting ways. It may be helpful to share one such journey that I undertook with my 11th-graders: a visit to Harvard University to hear Dr. Jocelyn Chadwick, the renowned Mark Twain scholar, give a lecture for us on *The Adventures of Huckleberry Finn* (Twain, 1885/2008). (The preparation for the trip included hoards of e-mails, lots of begging, pleading, and, okay, even some conniving, but the result was worth it all!)

The night before our field trip, I had set two alarms. The coffee timer was ready for 5:30 A.M., with a Jamaican roast waiting to be brewed. "One cup of this will have you buzzed for hours," my father had said. When I went to bed at 9:30, the old feeling of preparing for the first day of school as a little kid came back to me. I used to fold my first-day clothes and put them beside my bed; my backpack would be set with a new binder, pencils, calculator, and planner. I could never fall asleep right away—I'd lay there thinking about what teachers I'd have, who would be in my classes, and how cool I was (or wasn't). There was the irrepressible sense that tomorrow, my life would begin once more.

Again, that old feeling returned. Tomorrow, three other teachers, my father, and I were taking 140 high school juniors to Harvard University for a lecture on *The Adventures of Huckleberry Finn*. I couldn't fall asleep.

"Lukis! It's 5:31—what time did you say the kids are going to be arriving at the school? I've got the coffee going and I'm going to shower now. Are you showering this morning—and what are you wearing? Do I need to wear a shirt and tie or is it casual?" My father stood in the doorway of my old bedroom. It felt good to be in my parent's house again, this time as a guest.

We arrived at 6:52 A.M., and about 25 students were already there waiting.

"Mr. Reynolds, we've been here since 6:20!" I had told the kids to arrive between 6:50 and 7:10, and the onslaught of students who had had trouble sleeping that long were more awake than I'd ever seen them for first period class at 7:32. One by one, they came and introduced themselves to my father. My colleagues soon arrived, and within minutes 140 kids were signing in and boarding buses. John Walker was the lead bus driver, and he appeared to me like an old war vet who knew a lot but spoke a little. He seemed to be a mix of MacGuyver, Yoda, and Morgan Freeman.

John parked us along Appian Way in Harvard Square at 10:15 A.M. Rain was pelting us as we got off the bus. One colleague's umbrella acquiesced to the wind; if it could have spoken, it would have shouted in pain. The students fled forward, excited to be on their own in Cambridge, with no walls, intercoms, or bells.

Harvard students passed by this excited group of 140 high school juniors, and the quizzical looks on their faces said it all: *Who are you guys?* We soon ushered the students into the Harvard lecture hall, and a hush fell over them. Dr. Chadwick appeared and was all smiles; her energy could be felt immediately. She gave out hugs of greeting to the teachers, and within moments the lecture began.

Her booming voice filled the hall, and without a microphone she silenced any whisperings of our students. In the first 5 minutes, she had a number of them leaning forward in their seats, then laughing, then thinking, then questioning.

"Mr. Ray," Dr. Chadwick began with a student whose name she remembered from introductions, "if you became a very rich man, would you just decide to give it up—I mean not even for a charity or some possession—just give it up—throw it all away?"

"No, I wouldn't."

"Well, that's what Twain did. After writing the best-selling *Tom Sawyer*, Twain began part II, *Huck Finn*. He wrote five chapters, then took a 7-year break. When you write an essay, Ms. Elkey, how long do you take?"

"Hours, probably."

"Hours? Whoo—you need to come here. Twain took 7 years off his writing of the novel—would your teachers let you do that? The reason is, it became something Twain didn't realize: It wasn't about writing a best-seller, it was about writing the truth as he knew it. He wrote a novel with a message, and that message wasn't popular."

The conversation continued, with Dr. Chadwick asking questions, challenging the students, and always referring to them by their last names—"as a sign of respect" she told us afterward.

Two hours later, we regrettably had to cut the conversation and boarded the buses to make it back to school before the dismissal bell. On the ride home, some students slept, some watched movies, some listened to music, some were deep in thought. My father and I talked about Dr. Chadwick, the students, and how people learn best. He said he had loved Twain most of his reading life, but he learned things from Dr. Chadwick today he had never heard before.

After the three buses pulled into the high school parking lot, I stood outside the doors and said goodbye to each of the students. Big smiles, bright faces, and wet clothes made their way past me, saying "thank you" as they went. It felt as though we all would have stayed on those buses, at the lecture hall, or even in the wind and rain of Cambridge a whole lot longer.

CONCLUSIONS

Helping students learn how to think differently begins when we as teachers allow ourselves to think differently. We are under so many pressures and stresses, but we must commit ourselves to constant reminders of the passion, calling, and beliefs that first drove us into the English classroom in the first place. Language, meaning, literature, and love brought us to our classrooms. We sensed that such a place would afford us the space to allow our hearts to beat fast alongside those of our students.

We want to make a difference, feel alive, and prepare students to be passionately skillful and boldly themselves in a world that increasingly tries to inundate us all with consumerism and superficiality. So in order for our own creativity in teaching to be authentic, we must keep alive our own faculties of *compassion, imagination,* and *trust through experience.* We cannot live lives bereft of these three necessities and then expect our students to somehow learn to embody them.

As we allow these three to make inroads into our hearts, we also model for our students what their practice looks like. As we talk about any assignment, their presence becomes evident. As we introduce new concepts, assessments, and texts, students will hear in our tones and see on our faces the kind of compassion, imagination, and trust through experience that we hope they will come to embrace. When we vulnerably welcome these three faculties into our teaching, then the creative work we develop and explore with our students becomes not only a tool for their growth—it grows us, too.

GUIDING QUESTIONS

1. Which of the three faculties for changing ways of thinking, being, and seeing are you most drawn to? Why do you think this is so?
2. Which of the three do you find most difficult to practice in your own personal life, away from school? In other words, do you find yourself in relationships or situations where your compassion runs cold, your imagination runs dry, or you do not trust? Spend a few moments journaling about specific times when you have felt an absence of one of these three.
3. Can you think of a teacher you had as a student that embodied one or more of these faculties? Write a memory of that teacher. If the teacher is still alive, why not try to get an e-mail address and send a note—reconnect and glean from him or her some of the fire you seek.
4. Can you consider a short field trip with your students? Start small: Sketch some notes for a place to which you might travel that is nearby and that would be cost-effective. Enlist some other teachers to help you plan a trip.
5. Go back to the section "Imagination" in this chapter. Skip all my words, and read only the cited material. What lines jump out at you from other writers?
6. Can you recall ever telling an incredibly silly and ridiculous story? What was it about? To whom did you tell it? Why? Can you picture yourself capturing that same kind of giddiness and sharing it with your students—letting your guard down a bit with them, in other words?
7. If you have never told a completely ridiculous story—the kind that only makes sense to a 4-year-old—try telling one right now. If you need an audience, write it down and then e-mail it to me at LWReynolds@gmail.com. I promise I'll reply with an equally ridiculous response!

Final Reflections:
The Agony and the Sweat

WHEN I WAS in the 1st grade at John F. Kennedy elementary school in Windsor, Connecticut, I created my first "published" book. Our school had a publishing center where students from ages 5 through 11 could bring our tattered pages of tales and nice volunteer moms would type up the stories for us, bind the pages together with plastic coil, and then give us two copies of the book to illustrate. I titled my rambling, semicoherent, and effusive 30-page work *Life on Mars and Pluto*. It is still the piece of which I am most proud. Detailing the life of Be-Bop and Rock-Steady, the book follows the plot of evil King Jell-O as he tries to destroy the entire universe. As a subplot, the hero-protagonists also must rescue Penelope and Ginger, two beautiful maidens who just happen to be floating around the outer atmosphere of space.

I walked to school on the day I finished it, knowing I would drop off my revered manuscript into the hands of some smiling mother in the makeshift publishing house in one corner of the gymnasium. I knew that no matter how strange or irrelevant my content was, she would be rapturous: "Wow! This is a *great* idea!" Leaving the school, I wanted to write again, sensing the beautiful collision of two worlds: passion and creation.

In college, I decided to become a teacher for the same reason that many do: I had passion, and I wanted to change the world, *one child at a time*. I was big on dreams—creating them and chasing them. I believed that all things were possible, that anything could happen, and that the stars align to reveal your vision as soon as you've worked to achieve it. After a while in the profession, I have heard some of the most incredible discourse among my colleagues and students. All want their classrooms to thrive on passion. We are teachers because we want to feel alive; we want to create magical moments and empower our students, who, in turn, crave this conduit of intensity in their daily academic experience. However, the machinery of life (the worried parents, the American sense of drive and competition to not "fall behind" in the world, overstressed teachers, standardized tests, school rankings, financial concerns—the list is unending) causes an abrupt shift from passion and creativity to need. First-graders must one day become 5th-graders, and 5th-graders must one day become high school students. And in a moment of whispering, the desire to create and imagine becomes the need to score and achieve. The human heart, in all its weighted glory and passion, becomes a nonentity.

"You need to do this in order to get into college"; "This will score you a good job"; "This will ensure you a spot with a great salary"; "This will protect you from ever having to worry": These are the phrases I hear in the halls of the high school and in the halls of my students' minds, echoing to me in a thousand essays what they have already learned so well. I fear that William Faulkner's (1950) solemn condemnation in his Nobel Prize acceptance speech of 1949 has not been heeded: "The young man or woman writing today has forgotten the problems of the human heart in conflict with itself which alone can make good writing because only that is worth writing about, worth the agony and the sweat." In place of the conflicts of the human heart, we often become consumed with superficial tricks and techniques, boxes to check that don't necessarily equate with genuine growth through our writing. It's entirely plausible that we can read essays from our students that can earn As by acing the rubrics—and even write them ourselves in graduate courses or workshops—yet don't ever engage our souls. The goals we normally pursue during high school classes, college searches, and early careers in order to smooth out a path for our feet—are they worth the agony and the sweat? If we do not live our lives creatively and use our voices, we become numb to our own voices and the voices of our students. We find ourselves stranded in a life where we have no language to speak but the language of numbers and success. Instead of asking "What can I create?" the question becomes "What can I get?"

Students are learning this today from the earliest ages. About half a dozen years ago, I wrote a piece for *The Hartford Courant* entitled "Keeping Students Excited About Reading" (Reynolds, 2005) that described the need for an acceptance of a wider range of reading material in our classrooms, in refutation of a piece by Harold Bloom in which he argued that Stephen King was not a writer worth reading. In response to my piece, I received this fascinating note from a retired 1st-grade teacher:

> I was delighted when I read your editorial, "Keeping Students Excited About Reading," in *The Hartford Courant*. I agree completely. After almost 25 years of teaching elementary students, I saw many children "turned off" because of what they were asked to do while reading a book. I watched a 1st grader enjoying reading . . . however, the problem was he hated the reading he was supposed to do and had carefully covered the book he wanted to read (a much higher-level book) with the cover of his assigned reading book. He was "caught" because he was enjoying reading so much he laughed out loud! His punishment? He was not allowed to go to the library and take out books for 1 month. Lesson taught—it is not O.K. to enjoy reading.

Our question today is simply this: What are we passionate about? What in our lives makes our hearts beat fast? If it's *getting*, then we're too inundated by all the voices that commanded we get with the program—read the right books, write the right essays, go to the right colleges, and get the right jobs. The masquerade of it all is that there is no such thing as a right job or college or essay or book. The right thing is that which wakes us up to the power of words and helps us become the people we long to be. And the vaguest generality of this truth can be stronger in our physical and emotional beings than all the specific numbers and successes the world has to offer. Pushing through the pores of our skin, the only worthwhile sweat we ever feel is that which originates in our hearts.

May all our teaching be laced with the fire of creativity, the passion of our own voices and stories, and the rigor of effective and meaningful classroom experiences. And may we all attend the wedding of high standards and wild creativity, knowing full well that it can be a relationship based on passionate love as well as loyal commitment.

The Boston Photograph

On July 22, 1975, Stanley J. Forman was working in the newsroom of the *Boston Herald American* newspaper when a police scanner picked up an emergency: "Fire on Marlborough Street!" Forman rushed to the scene, where multiple fire crews were battling an intense blaze. There was a distress call for a ladder team to the rear of the building to help a stranded woman and child. Forman followed.

Climbing atop the fire truck for a better view, Forman instinctively began covering the events before him. As firemen on the scene focused on their work, Forman's attention was directed to a young woman, Diana Bryant, and a very young girl, Tiare Jones. Both were seeking help from a fireman, Bob O'Neil, located on the roof directly above them. O'Neil moved to the fire escape and motioned for the truck's ladder to be brought to them. The flames came closer and closer to the fire escape as Forman continued to shoot.

Then, at the very instant the ladder reached the trio, the fire escape gave way. O'Neil clung to the ladder, but Bryant and Jones fell helplessly. Forman snapped a last picture before turning away, knowing the bodies were falling to the ground. Diana Bryant was pronounced dead at the scene.

Diana Bryant (bottom) and Tiare Jones (upper) fall helplessly from the broken fire escape.
Photo: Stanley J. Forman (stanleyformanphotos.com)

The young girl lived. Despite a heroic effort, O'Neil knew he had been just seconds away from saving the lives of both. Forman's work captured a vivid scene where mere seconds had meant life or death.

Text excerpted from http://alt.tnt.tv/specials/moi/photo_boston.html

Name _____   Date _____

Members of My Group _____

Overview

You and the other three members of your group are no longer students. The four of you are now the editorial board for the *Boston Herald American*. Stanley Forman, a staff photographer, walks into your board meeting, and he hands you the photos of what he has captured.

You have 25 minutes to make a decision: Will you print the photos or not? The paper needs to be sent to press in the next hour, so this time limit is essential. As you discuss what decision you will make, be sure to think about all of the consequences. Here are some questions to ask as you talk within your group:

- What is the purpose of your newspaper?
- What do the readers of your newspaper want to see/read about?
- What are the moral and ethical standards of your newspaper?
- What messages will you send by choosing to print or not print the photos?

Within your groups, be honest with your ideas and opinions. Each group member should have a half-page of his or her own thoughts along with notes on what other group members share. After 25 minutes, you will stand as a group and notify the rest of the staff at the *Boston Herald American* of your decision, as well as address any problems or questions that the rest of the staff has. (Use the rest of this page for your notes.)

The Historical Decision Made by the *Boston Herald American* and Its Consequences

The editorial board at the *Boston Herald American* chose to print three of the pictures that Stanley Forman took that day. Afterward, there was indeed outrage by some of the paper's readership. Letters-to-the-editor poured in saying the decision was awful. These photos showed death as it was in the midst of happening, and this kind of graphic depiction was seen by some as a moral trespass.

However, others thought the photos delivered the honest news and showed what really happened. Also, the photos of the dilapidated fire escape giving way became powerful proof for the public of the bad fire safety standards in lower-income housing areas in the city of Boston.

The following year, Forman's sequence of photos from the tragic event garnered him the 1976 Pulitzer Prize in Spot News Photography.

Do you think the historical results vindicated Forman's shooting of the photos and the newspaper's decision to print them? Why or why not?

Imagine that you are Tiare Jones. How do you feel growing up knowing these photos capturing your mother's death have been published for all to see?

Love and Marriage?

Name _____   Date _____

Due: _____

After reading "What I Wish I Had Known About Marriage" by Kristin Armstrong, think carefully about the experiences and advice she shares. Write a one-page response to the following questions:

What is the purpose of marriage?
Do you think you will marry?

Before you start your page, consider and respond to these helpful additional questions, which may unlock some of your thinking. Try to write what first comes to mind rather than what you think you should write.

Do you think marriage is always beneficial for both partners?

Would you like to marry when you are young or older?

What would you say are the essential elements of a marriage?

Do you think that we—as a culture—hold on too tightly to our "Cinderella stories"?

Why do so many people (estimated at 50%) get divorced?

What are the reasons for which a couple should decide to marry?

When do you think a couple should call it quits before the wedding date arrives?

Do you see yourself happily married one day because of intense passion, similar interests, or other things?

Considering Janie, Considering You, Considering Love

Name _____   Date _____

Reflecting on *Their Eyes Were Watching God*

What expectations do you have for a love relationship?

What are Janie's expectations for love?

What is something that has gone wrong with one or more of your relationships?

What is wrong with Logan Killicks?

How would you describe the characteristics of a *Dud*?

Where do your expectations come from in terms of relationships? Janie's?

Listen to Mr. Reynolds's story of love and how he decided to risk being vulnerable with the woman to whom he proposed. The following poem, by W. B. Yeats, comes into play. Be ready for it. Then see if Mr. R. recites it without any mistakes.

Question to think about as you listen: What does it mean to love someone?

When You Are Old
by William Butler Yeats (1865–1939)

When you are old and gray and full of sleep
And nodding by the fire, take down this book,
And slowly read, and dream of the soft look
Your eyes had once, and of their shadows deep;

How many loved your moments of glad grace,
And loved your beauty with love false or true;
But one man loved the pilgrim soul in you,
And loved the sorrows of your changing face.

And bending down beside the glowing bars,
Murmur, a little sadly, how love fled
And paced upon the mountains overhead,
And hid his face amid a crowd of stars.

Something Left to Love?

A Raisin in the Sun and Making Words Matter

Name _____   Date _____

Directions

Below, find Mama's speech to Beneatha after her daughter roars that Walter is no good and that she cannot love him—*there is nothing left to love!* Walter has decided to sell the house back to Lindner and is on the verge of giving up on dreams and hope.

Go through the speech, and underline and circle lines that move you. Write notes about yourself, people you know, and life problems and joys in the margins.

After you read and annotate (mark up) the speech, think about a person to whom or about whom you could make a speech like this. Who in your life needs to know that you love them and will not give up on them—the way Mama won't give up on Walter? On a separate sheet, write your own version of Mama's speech referencing the person on your mind and in your heart.

I. Mama's Speech

There is always something left to love.
Have you cried for that boy today?
Not for yourself and the family
because we lost the money.
I mean for him.
And what he's gone through.
And God help him.
God help him, what it's done to him.
Child, when do you think is the time
to love somebody the most?
When he's done good and made things
easy for everybody?
That ain't the time at all.
It's when he's at his lowest . . .
. . . and he can't believe in himself

because the world's whipped him so!
When you starts measuring somebody . . .
  . . . measure him right, child.
Measure him right.
You make sure that
you done taken into account . . .
  . . . the hills and the valleys
he's come through . . .
  . . . to get to wherever he is. (Hansberry, p. 135)

Paideia (or Socratic) Seminar

Name _____   Date _____

"I prefer nothing, unless it is true." —Socrates

The Paideia Seminar is based upon a theory of learning practiced by Socrates. His mode of education consisted of talking with people who were either travelers to or citizens of Greece in a way that forced them to think and rethink their own ideas or initial understandings of something. Many people hated him for this because powerful leaders would often end up looking foolish when Socrates was through with them.

Today, we will have our first Socratic Seminar. This is the way it works:

- *The "teacher" shuts up.* Socrates believed that teaching is not a matter of lectures, or of passing information from one body to another. Instead, he believed that genuine knowledge is already *inside* the soul of a person. The teacher's job, then, was to ask the right questions to call it forth. A story about the mythic gods propounds this point.
- *The questions are presented.* Below, you'll see three questions. My job will be to facilitate your discussion of these questions. Each person must respond at some point to one of the questions. The idea is to get the ball rolling, during which time people can respond to another's comments *and* to the questions. Respond to one question fully before moving on to the next.
- *Textual support is a must.* In the Socratic Seminar, reasons must be given for your ideas. If you assert something, you must back it up with a line or passage from the story. As you present your point, you must alert others to the line or passage you are using, and then read it aloud.
- *At the close, everyone notes where he or she stands.* The questions we deal with are pointed ones, and by the end of the class, the Socratic Seminar allows for those who want to change their position.
- *Listening is a MUST.* In order to have a good seminar, each member must listen to the comments of others. When you address someone's remark, refer to them by name and briefly restate their comment and then your addition to it.

Socratic Seminar
The Skin I'm In by Sharon G. Flake

Name _____   Date _____

As we discussed in class, a Socratic Seminar is a forum where there is no right answer—however, your ideas must be backed up by evidence from the text, your own experience, or connections to other texts or events.

Socrates believed that by asking questions and thinking out loud in the context of a community, people could get closer to what is true. Remember that your grade for this Socratic Seminar depends on your preparation (notes, talking points) and what you share in our discussion.

Here are the three questions we'll discuss in our Socratic Seminar. For each question, on a separate sheet, you should write:

- your ideas about the question
- lines from the book (with their page numbers) that back up your ideas
- other connections, events, or experiences

Be SURE to include all three of the above requirements before our discussion!

1. What do you think Maleeka should do about Char and John-John?

2. Agree or disagree with the following statement: Students should always talk to teachers when they are being bullied or hurt.

3. Why do many people make fun of what is different from them?

The Marriage of Passion and Purpose

(Yes! In a Critical-Analytical Thesis Essay! Hold the Phone!)

Name _____   Date _____

You have written a thesis statement, which you will use to argue passionately for your case in *The Great Gatsby*. Granted, you are not Tom Cruise or Demi Moore. (Or are you? I checked my class list very carefully, just on the notion that Tom Cruise might sign up for my course. But I was pretty sure I didn't see his name. In fact, now that I think about it carefully and seriously, I am sure he is not in this course.) So, having established that PEARL OF TRUTH (here used to represent the phrase "pearl of wisdom"), I can now move forward: You can be *like* Tom Cruise's character in *A Few Good Men*.

Argue passionately for what you believe about the ideas we discussed from the novel.

So that's the desired outcome, the goal, the promised land, the finish line, the pot of gold at the end of the rainbow, the ice cold drink of water after a long race, the "goodnight sweetheart" of every proverbial high school classroom, the victory.

But in Order to Get There . . .

The essays must have evidence! (Insert loud battle cry here—image: Mel Gibson and his slew of soldiers fighting to free Scotland from the tyranny of injustice. Our battle is for evidence. I will bring war paint tomorrow.) Imagine if Tom Cruise's character in *A Few Good Men* had simply stated his opinion—nothing much would have come of it. His evidence proved the case. In our essays, we must choose good evidence to support our thesis statements.

With the worksheet provided, you will gather six quotes that may be used to *prove your thesis*. Explore the novel and find six quotes and record them below. After each quote, include the page number in parentheses, followed by a period after the closing parenthesis (MLA format).

Essay Theme (What idea does your thesis focus on?):

    My Thesis Statement:

1.

2.

3.

4.

5.

6.

My Ideal Country

A Project in Conjunction with *I Have Lived a Thousand Years* by Livia Bitton-Jackson

Overview

In her Holocaust memoir, Livia Bitton-Jackson describes the way in which she and other Jewish people were subjected to gruesome treatment at the hands of Nazi soldiers in a country where injustice, discrimination, and fear had become the way of the world with Hitler in charge.

Now, imagine YOU are in charge of a country and your mission is to create a society that is the complete opposite. In other words, your goal is to craft a country where the laws, the people, the government—anything that is important to a functioning country—are as ideal and as fair as possible. Your mission is to create YOUR IDEAL COUNTRY.

Necessary Components of the Project

This is a big task. In order to make your mission clearer, below are the key requirements and due dates for the different parts of the project:

- *Write at least 10 laws that will govern your society*. Each law must be at least two complete sentences long, and it must be clearly explained and work to make your society more just and more ideal. Put your 10 laws on a separate page, and entitle them your country's **BILL OF RIGHTS**.
- *Choose and create all of the following*: (1) A name for your country, along with a five-sentence paragraph explaining why you chose that particular name and how it relates to the culture of your country. (2) Decide on a population for your country (how many people live there?); for a reference point, Germany had a population of 55 million people at the time of the Holocaust. (3) Create a map of your country, in color, that shows how big it is, what bodies of water are in or near it, what types of land there are within your country, and any other important facts.

71

- *What type of government will your country have?* Will there be a king or a queen? Will there be a legislature, as in America? Explain how your country will be governed on a separate sheet of paper; write at least two paragraphs.
- *What will the system of education be like in your country?* Will all children be required to go to school? If so, for how long? How many days of the year? Why? What subjects will students be required to study? Will there be college education? What will the teachers be like? Describe an average school day for an average student in your country. This section should be at least two full pages long.
- *What kinds of jobs will exist in your country?* List 15 different jobs that your country will need, and provide the salary for each job. For instance, in your ideal society—the country you create—will a baseball player make $30,000 while a social worker makes $200,000? Or vice versa? After listing the 15 jobs and the salary for each, write a paragraph describing why you made these choices at the bottom of this page.
- *What will your country's system of crime and punishment be like?* What will happen to people who break the 10 laws in your Bill of Rights? Write one page describing this process.
- *Who will be honored and revered in your country?* Write one page explaining your ideas.
- *Write a **Mission Statement** for your country.* This will be somewhat like the Declaration of Independence for America. Your **Mission Statement** will include: why your country is the (or at least your) ideal society; the values your country respects and strives toward; an example of how your country is a place of justice and equality (you can make up a story, inventing citizens in your country and using them as examples); anything else you want to include. This **Mission Statement** will be two pages long.

We will present our Ideal Countries in class during the week of _____. You will have a lot of time in class to work on your ideal countries, as we read *I Have Lived . . .* at home. I can't wait to see your countries! Be creative, break out of "The Cave," and be specific, clear, and honest in your work!

Good luck!

I Am Because

Essay on Self and Society

Due: _____

Overview

Think about what in society has influenced who you are at this very moment: Commercials? Friends? The way your parents treat each other? The absence of parents? Teachers? Which decisions can you confidently say are completely your own, and which decisions arise from the words, advice, demands, persuasions, or examples of others?

Specifics

This essay assignment asks you to dig deep into your own formation. How did you become the person that you are right now? Before writing your essay, take time to consider what messages have impacted your life and where these messages have come from. Also, consider moments in your life when you felt especially afraid, excited, jealous, ecstatic, or confused. Do moments of extreme emotion double as a formative crossroads?

Outline for Essay

This piece should be **three *full* pages, double-spaced**. It can be no longer and no shorter. For some of us, this may mean revising our words down to the barest essentials; for others of us, it may mean working hard to elaborate the page and a half we've been able to etch.

Begin by discussing your present state: How would you define yourself right now (consider gender, place, work, abilities, relationships, passions, non-negotiables)?

Then transition into making a *claim* about your formation. For example: I have resisted the influences of my society to become the person I **wanted** to become. Or perhaps: I can see how my identity has often been molded by the way my society has influenced me. Be original and honest with your claim.

Next, support your claim by using specifics—exactly *what* influences have been so important in shaping who you are, **or**, exactly *what* influences have you been able to resist? Has your resistance become an influence in itself?

Finally, discuss the influences in your life using ETHOS, PATHOS, and LOGOS. For each influence you mention, show why you would categorize it as an influence through ETHOS (someone or something with credibility, e.g., an authority figure, a hero, etc.), PATHOS (the influence appealed to your emotion—making you laugh, cry, desire, feel inadequate, etc.), or LOGOS (how the influence seemed to make logical sense to you, etc.). **Be sure to mention these terms TWICE EACH as you write your essay!**

Audience and Grading

For this essay, I am your audience. I hope you will be honest and that you'll be able to do some excavating of your past. My goals for you in writing this piece are twofold:

1. You will gain a clearer understanding of how ethos, pathos, and logos function in yourselves and in our society on multiple levels—including an understanding of how many pressures are at work to try to persuade us to think and behave in certain ways.
2. You will be able to step outside of the immediate cries for your attention to reflect on who you are, the decisions you have made, and how much society has informed those decisions.

Since speaking with conviction demands that writing be clear, meaningful, and powerful, I will be grading your work based on the questions below:

1. Is the essay COMPLETELY FREE of any errors in grammar, spelling, and punctuation?
2. Does the essay practice all the principles of writing on the handout from class?
3. Does the essay use the terms ETHOS, PATHOS, and LOGOS at least TWO TIMES (each)?
4. Does the essay explain how different influences in society use ethos, pathos, and logos?
5. Is the essay authentic (honest, engaging, and incorporating a clear voice)?
6. Is the essay stapled?

If the answers to ALL of the above questions are YES, then the essay will receive a grade of A+. If the answers to 5 of the 6 questions are YES, then the paper will receive a B+. If the answers to 4 of the 6 questions are YES, then the paper will receive a C+.

3 of 6 = C–	1 of 6 = D–
2 of 6 = D+	0 of 6 = F

Encouragements

You have a voice unlike any other. The words you share become your trademark, your way of seeing the world around you—making meaning that matters to you and to those who read your words. When you write an essay, you engage in an exercise of speaking with conviction. I will treat your words as sacred things; I will read them carefully, and I am honored to receive them. I believe that what you have to share is worthwhile, and I will treat it with respect, honesty, and engage with you in conversation so that we both might learn.

Do You Live Like a Crab?

Name _____   Date _____

Overview

Fishermen say that when they catch crabs, they can keep them in buckets without any coverings at all! When asked why they don't worry about the crabs escaping by clawing their way up the sides to freedom, the fishermen usually reply that the other crabs simply pull their peers right back down into the bucket. In other words, if most of the crabs see that another crab is making its way up the side of the bucket, they'll claw at this crab until it falls back into captivity.

Theme Statement

The majority of crabs will not let another crab escape to freedom, life, and peace if they can't have it or do it themselves.

Connection

In school—and especially in the 7th grade—it is often not "cool" to look smart, to act like you know something, or show that your ideas are strong. Sometimes your classmates will be like those crabs in the bottom of the bucket, and they will try to pull you back down because you are succeeding and because you are working hard to gain freedom, peace, and growth!

Your Mission

In your own words, and with as much honesty as possible, explain how the above metaphor works in your own life. Give at least three different examples of how you see this playing out (or, if you don't see it, offer three examples of why you think you *don't* see this idea playing out in your own life).

Use the questions below to help your thinking, and write your response on white-lined paper and then staple it to the back of this sheet and hand it in. Be sure to include your name and the date!

Guiding Questions

- Who in your life tries to pull you back down when you have success?
- Where do you feel the most pressure to remain at the bottom of the bucket?
- Have you ever climbed out of the bucket, even though others told you to stay?
- What are your dreams—and how will you reach them even if other people want you to fail?

Losing Sight of the Shore

"In order to discover new lands, you must lose sight of the shore for a very long time."

—André Gide, French writer

So far in your high school career, your writing has dealt mainly with other people's work. You have constructed critical-analytical essays (which are crucial to learning), made predictions about other writers' novels and their conclusions, and written letters to characters within works.

Now, you will create your own.

Leaving the shores you are used to may be exciting for some, scary for others, and even relentlessly confusing.

In constructing your novella, you will learn how to write effective sentences, use vivid details, clearly reveal a scene, and create realistic and powerful, funny dialogue.

I will warn you now: At times it is going to seem silly, even stupid, to try to make your characters do something interesting. At other times, you may feel as though you're banging your head against a wall, and that activity may actually begin to sound appealing. (When this happens, walk away from your novella and drink some orange juice instead of performing said activity. I recommend Minute Maid's orange/passionfruit mix; it's got mango in it.)

But I promise you: If you continue to work on it each week, as proposed below, when the end of the year comes around, you will hold in your hands a 30- to 50-page work of which you can be infinitely proud.

Guidelines

- Your final novella must be between 30 and 50 pages (see me if you want to write more): typed, double-spaced, 12-point font (Palatino is a nice book print font).
- Your novella should have a title and a cover page.
- Your novella should be about anything you want it to be about. There are no limits.
- The work must be original, your own, and about something you are interested in.

Due Dates and Work Times

- Each Friday, you will bring in two new pages (typed) of your novella. You should keep your work on the same disk, CD, or one of those little thingeys you insert into a computer that I do not have because they cost too much and therefore I do not know the name of them. Hand in the typed pages to me, and keep the disk yourself.
- Save a second copy of EVERYTHING you write on your school account, too.
- Sometimes we will use a class period to work on our novellas, so always have your disk or a current copy of your novella on your school drive.
- We will use Fridays to **workshop** your new material.
- You may meet with me *at any time* to talk about your artistic decisions or roadblocks.

AAAAAAAHHHHHHH!
(Or, Notes on Beginning a Novella)

Name _____   Date _____

Brain fart? Your mind playing wall ball with ideas? Lots of hot air and only the window fogging up? Not sure how to start? Not sure if you want to start? Not sure if you *really* want to even be in Mr. Reynolds's class anymore? Not sure if there really is a *whole, entire company* (!) devoted solely to making the plastic tops that come on cups of soda at fast-food joints?

Stop! Cease and desist all worries!

Read this quote:

"Wisdom begins with wonder." Socrates said that. Really. I heard him say it just after I watched Napoleon storm Brussels (did he ever storm Brussels or am I just making that up?).

So to start your tale, you've really only got to do one thing: *wonder*.

Wonder about everything. Wonder about why a mom is yelling at her 3-year-old boy at the grocery store. (Ah! There's a start to your novella: "The tired mother held her son's shirt and yelled at him. She was trying to buy lettuce, and her son was trying to be Superman. The desires didn't mix . . . " and take it from there.)

Wonder about who the heck *actually* cleans the classrooms when we all go home. Make up a story about it. Here's a start: "His name was Jonathan, and he had once wanted to be an astronaut. . . . " Then tell his life story and how he ended up as a janitor. Did a true love cheat on him? Did he do it because the money was good?

Wonder about words. Words like *gargantuan* (big), *osmosis* (I still remember the word from AP Biology—why is that? It must be a cool stinking word), *fleeting* (leaving or disappearing quickly), and *soothing* (another cool word).

Start your story with an action: "The dog slowly removed its jaws from the man's inner thigh . . ." and continue. Why did the dog bite the man? What was he doing? Newspapers? Robbery? Trying to train his own dog?

or

"The mailman delivered the letter, and that's when she knew it couldn't be undone. It was there. He would read it . . . " What was the letter about? Was it to her father, whom she had hated all her life for something he did? Was it to a boyfriend, mother, long-lost friend? Use your novel to tell the woman's life story and what the letter is all about.

Start your story with a description of a character. Today, look closely at everyone, everywhere you go: Pick a person you think looks interesting, and just start describing him or her: "She wore black pants and a black bow on the back of her hair. Her face seemed light, almost as if there was a set of bulbs in a layer behind her skin, lighting up all the pores of her tissue. . . . "

or

Use a quote to start your novella: "What in the hell! How could you say that! Ever since I was a young man, all I ever wanted to do was make good on my dreams, and now you have the nerve to tell me *this*?!" Keep it going: What has he been told? Who told it to him? Where are the people talking? Are they lovers, friends, married, older, younger? Write the dialogue and let it take you where it will.

or

Start your novel with a setting. Just start describing a place: "The path was all dirt, with the occasional rock lying in the middle of it. Every time you looked forward, the path would seem to just go on forever. The trees around seemed to hang down, as if their heads were lowered, giving way to the fact that they had lost against whoever stormed the woods to make a trail. They were green and . . ." dying? newly born? fresh? Keep it going—keep describing the trail. Then, who is on the trail? Why are they walking it? Are they friends, on a mission, looking for someone?

or

Write a novel using your own life as fodder. What's going on with you? Who have you been hanging out with? Who have you been interested in? What has made you mad or happy or sad or excited?

Ultimately, the start of your novel may not even be the start you keep! It may be just a way to get to some good stuff. But don't worry. Just start writing something, anything. Get it down on paper and bring it in on Friday, and we'll take it from there.

Copy any of the starts I've used above. Grab one and just run with it! Take it! It's yours! Whatever you need to do, do it. Get going.

Keep this in mind as you write:

Writing creatively is about opening up a part of yourself that may have been quieted for a long time. Either because we've told you to think critically for so long that you've forgotten how to write whatever you want, OR because you're so busy and anxious with life that you can't get to that place where you let your soul breathe.

And that's all writing is, just letting your soul have a nice long walk or run or hike or whatever is most relaxing for you. Before you try to write, put some of your favorite music on, think your best thoughts about who you are and what your dreams are, and then go for it.

If you're having trouble because of boyfriend or girlfriend issues, or lack thereof, or because of anxieties about grades or colleges—write it! Start writing about a character very much in the spot you're in! You are a master of the blank page. Whatever happens, even if what you are putting down is so crappy that you have to laugh, well, then laugh and keep writing. Tell yourself, "No matter what, I'll get two pages." Then, if it helps, make a sound like a pirate and wear a one-eyed patch, and keep writing. It's not like I do anything like that, though. But I will tell you something that I do do. (Hey, I didn't say "doo-doo" there, okay—so don't even think about it like that. I meant it as in "something that I do try—I do do. But one day maybe I will show you a short story that I wrote entitled "The Wad." I wrote it when I was in college, and it's about exactly what you think it's about.)

When I write, I put on my Boston Red Sox hat. I also roll up my sleeves, put on a CD that I like, and sit down at the computer. The hat is a physical thing I do to let myself know, "Alright, buddy, it's time to write." Believe it or not, it helps.

I don't know if any of this helps you, though I hope at least one thing gets you thinking. If you've got a hat, try it. Or try something completely uniquely you—just do something to tell yourself that you're not going to dwell on grades, college, romantic roadblocks, or any other anxious things that may keep your butt plastered to the couch rather than the seat at your computer. Get up and start writing something— anything—and have fun while you do it.

I can't wait to read them!!

On a separate sheet, record a few ideas regarding characters, plots, problems, situations, and voices that interest you.

Mr. Reynolds's
(Things to Look Out for While You Write and Revise or Else He'll Make Lots of Huge Pen Marks All Over Your Page to Alert You to Them)
List of Writing Rules

Save this in a special place, alongside your love letters, pearl earrings, Mickey Mantle baseball card, or lucky shoelace

1. Vary sentence structure: Do not begin three sentences in a row with the same word (*The, The, The . . . I, I, I*).
2. Use specific examples to show rather than tell:

    - dialogue
    - experiences
    - action
    - description

3. Short sentences can be combined. Together, they can create long sentences. These long sentences are still grammatically correct. They are flowing. They prevent the reader from having to halt again and again. Combining short sentences to form long, grammatically correct sentences that flow creates an ease for the reader, preventing him or her from halting again and again.
4. Put commas and periods inside quotation marks, semicolons outside.
5. As you revise your sentences, scan for repeated words and phrases, then give them a kick in the arse. For example, look at this sentence:

    > Holden's problem is one of fear. The problem is a problem because it is problematic in his life and his family's. The problem with the problem is that it poses a problem for Holden's ability to connect with people.

    Using the same phrase again and again is either (a) very annoying and weak writing or (b) a cover-up for a writer who does not know what he or she wants to say.
6. Watch out for comma splice run-ons: These occur when a writer places a comma in between two phrases that can stand alone.

> Dogs represent the proverbial passive-aggressive nature, cats represent the manic-depressive nature.

Instead, use a semicolon because both of these phrases can stand alone. Or use a transition word after the comma like *and* or *while*.

> Dogs represent the proverbial passive-aggressive nature, and cats represent the manic-depressive nature. (This line uses a transition word.)

> Dogs represent the proverbial passive-aggressive nature; cats represent the manic-depressive nature. (This line uses a semicolon.)

7. Now, for real, yo, watch out for all kinds of stuff that's okay for how we might talk, but not for what we write. Word. We got to write with precision, dawg. Keep it tight; keep it clear.

8. When referring to people in a sentence, use *who*, not *that*. For example:

> Jehoshaphat and Agnes are two people *that* I really like. (This is wrong.)

> Jehoshaphat and Agnes are two people *that* I really like, a lot. (This is still wrong.)

> Jehoshaphat and Agnes are two people *whom* I really like because they have the coolest stinking names I've ever heard. (This is correct.)

9. When it comes to good writing, William Faulkner once said, "Kill your darlings." Even the sentences that we fall in love with may be wordy and confusing. Keep everything focused; say only what needs to be said.

10. REVISE!!! Read your piece over many times, and read it OUT LOUD. Speaking the words helps us hear where sentences may be awkward or run-ons.

11. **Always use present tense verbs when writing about literature!**
NO: The boy was afraid because the bullies continued beating him up.
YES: The boy *is* afraid because the bullies *continue* beating him up.

12. Titles of short stories and poems should be in quotes: "The Street" and "The Road Not Taken." Titles of novels, movies, and plays should be in italics or underlined: *Of Mice and Men, Death of a Salesman, The Shawshank Redemption*.

13. READ YOUR PIECE OUT LOUD!!

Writing Authentic Dialogue

Name _____   Date _____

Overview

As we discussed in class yesterday, dialogue is one of the ways an author SHOWS rather than tells us information, emotion, and plot. You'll have a chance to practice writing one page of real, authentic, WOW, thick-as-honey-and-free-as-a-butterfly dialogue tonight for homework. It doesn't have to be perfect, but you're working hard to SHOW ideas, emotions, and plot rather than use a narrative voice to TELL the reader.

Below, check out my own example of one page of dialogue. It's not perfect, but you can see the writer in me working hard to SHOW instead of . . . yup . . . NO TELLING!

"So, how's the new apartment working out?" My father had phoned for the third time in three days. He had retired after a long career in the insurance business and had fondly said only weeks before, "Now I'm gonna have nothing to do except come over and see you and Jen!"

"It's really good so far, and it's slowly getting more and more organized." I sniffed a couple of times and blew my nose.

"Your allergies are still bothering you, huh? Have you gotten a vacuum yet?"

"No, Dad, not yet, but we're going to go to Bed, Bath and Beyond and pick something up later in the week." I sneezed, and I could almost see my father shudder.

"Alright, Lukis, Lukis-a-reno, you've got to get a vacuum with Hepa capabilities. Hepa is where it's at, Lukis. Hep-a! Hep-a! You've got to get one of those babies."

"Alright Dad-o, we'll pick up a Hepa vacuum cleaner—"

"Hep-a! Hep-a! It's all about the Hepa, big guy."

I knew my father was almost lost, so with all the resolve I could muster, I tried to change the subject.

"Hey Dad-o are you and Mom going on date night to the Bushnell this weekend?"

"Hep-a babes! Whoo, you've got to get a Hep-a. That thing will wipe the dust mites right out of those carpets. After you use a Hep-a vacuum it'll feel like dyin' and goin' to Heaven."

I was quiet for a moment. If he were here, Harry Wilson Reynolds III would have grabbed me by the shoulders and squeezed. He would have tried to do a Hepa vacuum dance. I shuddered.

"Dad, I think Jen needs me for a minute." Jen was out at the grocery store.

"Alright, but are you gonna buy a Hep-a vacuum cleaner? You need to get one of those!!"

"Dad-o, I love you, Big D."

"Love you too, babes. Hepa!"

We hung up. The next day, while I was at school setting up my classroom, my father came over with a red Kenmore vacuum and vacuumed the entire apartment for 2 hours. Jen couldn't stop him. Arriving home that day, I had no allergy problems, and when we went to bed, Jen asked, "Did you know that the vacuum your father bought us is a Hepa model?"

Your Task

Write **one page**, double-spaced, of dialogue that you had this summer. The above is a model.

- Indent each time a new character speaks.
- The conversation can be with two or more people. No conversations talking to yourself (yet, anyway).
- Include details about the people involved: their emotions, attitudes, physical descriptions if in person.
- Be creative, B-E Creative, B-E-C-R-E-A-T-I-V-E! Whoo! Whoo-ah! (Re-read this last requirement while doing a cheer of your own choreographic invention.)

Brief, Personal Writing Prompts

Note to Readers: These writing prompts have been very successful with high school and college students. They include connections to the lives of students, yet in ways that challenge them to think more broadly about reactions, responses, and their own hypothetical ability to handle situations. They can be used in class, used for homework, or expanded into longer creative works.

Someone very close to you dies. Who is it? How do you respond, and how does this affect your dreams, visions of the American Dream, and life as a whole?

You are driving home late one night and a drunk driver swerves and hits you. Your car is totaled, and you are in the hospital with serious injuries. Who is with you, and how do you handle the situation? The driver of the other car is also alive, and doctors say he would like to speak with you. What happens?

You become engaged. Who is the lucky man or woman, and how did the proposal go? How does this change your life?

You find out that you are pregnant or have impregnated someone else. Who is the father/mother? What do you plan to do about this situation?

You receive a promotion at work. What is the promotion, and what are your plans for your career path considering this promotion?

You lose three things very close and important to you. What are the three things, and what do you plan to do now that they are lost?

You may choose to have any three things you want. These can be very tangible or very intangible. What are they, and how did you get them?

On a long-distance (collect) phone call made to you last night, someone shared some earth-shattering news with you. What is the news, who was the person, and how does this change your life from here on out?

Last night, while you were watching *American Idol*, there were several urgent news interruptions. Something huge has happened that affects the world. What is it, and what do you do about it?

You father dies. Write about who he was as a person, your relationship with him, and what you think about your own life now that this has happened.

You took a HUGE risk yesterday. It was one of the biggest and hardest things you've ever done. What was it, why did you take it, and what do you do now?

A close relative leaves her child on your doorstep, literally. She leaves you a note in rhyming couplets:

> Here is little Johnny,
> I can't be his Mommy.
> He's too tough for me,
> Please help me, see,
> I can't take the care
> That he needs to bear.

What do you do with the child? How does this change your view of life?

There is a huge crime committed in your hometown. It affects most of the members of the community, and many people are involved. What is it, and how does it affect your view of life?

You win the lottery. How much do you win? What do you do with the money? How does it affect your view of life?

You do something unbelievably great. This thing you do is so miraculous, so wonderful, so amazing that newspapers are beginning to write stories about it, and television programs are beginning to call. What is this thing you've done, and how will it change you?

You are wrongly accused of committing a crime. What crime have the police arrested you for, and why do you think they accused you instead of the person who really did it? How do you plan to get out of this mess? How does this affect your vision of America?

You have invented something. In your spare time, it just came to you. You patented it, and now it's on the market. What is it? Why did you do it? How much money are you making?

You did something very, very, very stupid. You are now apologizing to everyone you love. What was it, and why did you do it? Will people forgive you?

Listening to Random Thoughts

Name _____   Date _____

Overview

As we discussed in class and read from Anne Lamott, sometimes we need to open the floodgates of our minds in order to produce pearls of great beauty in our writing. As you prepare for YOUR OWN chance to record every thought and idea your brain processes, take a look through mine. Many are incredibly goofy. Some are serious. Some are in poetic form, others in prose, and there are even quotes that crossed my mind. Remember, anything goes here. Who knows—an idea or a line or a thought might be born that will become the seed for a great story, essay, or poem!

Mr. R.'s Random Thoughts (1 Hour)

Eating cereal at night is romantic to me. Those slowly softening cinnamon-touched flakes embody all that a good romance should be. And when, in front of the window sill, I stare out into the night sky, I wonder if—just maybe—you're not also chomping on a bowl of LIFE cereal.

"Melodies heard are sweet, but those unheard are sweeter." A great poet quipped these lines. I cannot remember the name of this great poet. Is it because the name is not what matters?

Jell-O, baby. It's all about the Jell-O. Green, red, and yellow. What a beautiful world.

And standing there in the hot twilight, I knew things would never be the same. *Damn*, I thought.

Don't feed me that line of crap. I want to know what really makes you tick.

If you really want to know, then, it's something I can't explain, but it is embodied every time I see a pair of birds swoop through the sky together. It's funny, but even when they're alone, birds never seem lonely. Why is that?

Tree leaves, bee stings, and why doesn't my landlady always put her car in the garage?

"My definition of poetry, if I were forced to give one, would be this: words that become deeds." —Robert Frost

Besides the air being
Cooler, driving at night makes
Me feel rebellious.

Slicing along the highway,
You got to hate it, when the napkin breaks
And the mucus slides all over your hand.

Baby hands grab hard.
Big people grab harder,
Cry longer,
And when our hands are pried open,
We pretend they were never clenched.

Fists are useful things
Inside a huge can of grape jelly,
Because then the stickiness would stay
Out of the insides of your hands.

"In moments of ecstasy and joy, we all wish we had a tail we could wag."
—W. H. Auden

Really, what is the point of bumper stickers?
Bumping into one another, what is the point of being real?
Sticking is usually not a good thing,
But sometimes, it's all we've got.
So let's keep reading each other's bumpers.

If there were a world where oranges were the only food, then I would enjoy danc-ing with the people of that world. Also, I would, out of common courtesy, not ask them about apples.

When we've got to sneeze, it'd be nice to really let it all out.

As for coughing, I say, go for it.

Lying on the ground, looking up at the stars,
Maybe the neighborhood kid comes by.
We say hello to him, to his dog.
Then we feel a bit better about ourselves.

We wonder about what is right and what is wrong,
Taking tiny steps along
Sidewalks with caution signs all over them.
What if we ran in the fields instead?

Bursting forth, we are babies every moment of our lives if we are alive at all.

The only thing I can say about all that is, can you repeat it—this time slowly, and while spinning around in circles?

If I were to open up my own deli, I would call it "Ham It Up."

Confidence is like an old bird watching the chicks fly. They're swooping all over the place, hollering, revealing themselves. When they're tired, he then silently slices the air, and with one long motion like the steady stroke of a pen across a blank page, makes them all gape.

Flavors are often fruits. Grape, Orange, Banana, Strawberry. Has anyone ever thought of making new flavors that do not exist? Some could be: Wanoma, Hogelu, and Gumojo. Not only would this give people more options to choose from, but it would also free up the fruits to do more productive work, perhaps.

The purpose of writing—ah, I am not sure about that. Do we write because we have to, want to, or for the growth of our world and its people? If we write for any of these reasons, maybe we end up writing for them all.

The thing I wonder about Adam and Eve is: Did they fight? Did they disagree a lot?

What can we say about people who do not wear deodorant? Well, we can surely say that it is their prerogative. However, it still affects us. Is that like seat belts? No. But it must be like something, because everything is like something.

Gum is an interesting thing. We have taken all the knowledge of our species and invented something that causes our mouths to consistently open and close at a semiconstant rate for long periods of time without rest. And we pay for the ability to do this.

Appearances take up a lot of time, thought, and comparison. This is energy that could be well spent in a variety of different ways. For example, if I spend 20 minutes thinking about how I compare to the guy in the movie, I could have been writing my own screenplay for a new movie. And that is an idea I am not too proud of, nor am I sure why it even made it onto my random thoughts list. In fact, it could be the worst random thought I have ever had. It is nowhere near as interesting, or thoughtful, or even as honest as most of the other thoughts I have had. And now look at what I have done: wasted plenty of time comparing that last random thought to the other random thoughts when I could have been writing lots of new ones.

The safest place I can think of is lying between my parents when I was 2 or 3 years old and had woken up from a nightmare or there was a thunderstorm or something. I remember climbing in between those two big bodies, sleeping so easily, and as soon as I got in, it felt like my own little cave. A trench in the warfare of a 2-year-old's life. And I manned my trench well. It's cool to think that soon I may be a part of my own son's safe place.

Windows: glasses for people with really big eyes.

What if every time a teacher gave a quiz, it was an official rule that the teacher also had to say a tongue-twister? For example, "Alright, class, I hope that you've studied diligently and prepared well for your quiz on 18th-century French lifestyles. Close your books and I will pass out the quiz. And also, Peter Piper picked a peck of pickled peppers. Good luck." I think that some students would do better on their quizzes. But it would also confuse a lot of students.

Maybe the way to be a good teacher is to be crazier than any of your students. For example, every time a student did something crazy, the teacher would do a crazier thing right back. Here's how a scenario might play out: Student A throws a pencil at Student B. Teacher sees incident. Teacher throws a cream pie at Student A. Oh, I forgot to mention that for this idea to work, the school board would have to agree to fund the purchase of lots of cream pies, and maybe other things like Burger King hats (although there is a chance that those could be donated), tricycles, and lots of clap-on lighting.

I think, perhaps, that a beautiful thing can be beautiful in lots of different ways. One way is its form, its shape. But another way is its presence. Not the thing itself, but a *sense* of the thing. A. E. Housmann once said, "Poetry is not the thing said, but a way of saying it." I remember the day I found that quote. I was buried in the stacks of a little, out-of-the-way library in Oxford.

Socrates said, "Wonder is the beginning of wisdom." I like that.

Okay, this is Mr. R. writing to you, my 11th-graders, again. My rational mind is writing to all of your rational minds. But now, get ready to be very *non*rational. Spend 1 hour letting your mind record anything and everything it wants to. Your rational mind is moving out of the driver's seat, and in comes your Highly Creative Really Cool Though Never Having Much Time To Process Mind.

GO!

Introduction to Anthology Project
(Example from Actual Book, 7th-Grade Students)

Robert Frost once said, "No tears in the writer, no tears in the reader." It was his way of suggesting that if a writer is not passionately interested in the words she is putting onto the page, then the reader will be indifferent as well.

In my 7 years of teaching, I have seen my fair share of disinterested students, launching questions toward the front of the classroom such as, "Mr. Reynolds, why do we have to write about *this*?" in that complaintive, sing-song way that only students possess. My answer has generally been, "Because it will help you in your next step in life (fill in the blank with *college, high school, the latest standardized test, etc.*)." However, perhaps more than preparation for their next steps in life—or at least just as much as—students also need opportunities to express who they are *now* and what they think, feel, and believe *now*. Indeed, as Frost might say, students need chances to write things of their own choosing, and about which they care: whether in ways serious or silly.

Essentially, this volume of essays, stories, and poems is just such a book. It has been crafted and created entirely by my students, and they have chosen their own topics and formats through which to pursue their interests in life and writing.

Additionally, we wanted the funds from this volume to benefit a cause outside ourselves. More than anything in these early years of the 21st century, students—as well as those who have long since said farewell to the classroom—need to comprehend the great responsibility that is ours on the world stage: that our individual and collective passions, strengths, and dreams should always possess the ability to aid another. Mark Twain's words are best invoked toward this end: "To get the full value of joy, you have to have someone to share it with."

Therefore, all of the proceeds raised by the sale of this little volume will benefit a charity which the students overwhelmingly chose to support through this year's writing: Free the Slaves.

Currently, there are an estimated 27 million slaves worldwide. This staggering number includes those victims of sex trafficking, child slavery, and family bondage, where many people are kept against their will to make their owners rich. Kevin Bales, the world's foremost expert on this tragic blight of slavery, founded Free the

Slaves to work to stop slavery worldwide. His work focuses on freeing existing slaves, and also on helping others become aware of the tragedy of its current existence. If you are interested in learning more, please visit: www.freetheslaves.net.

Ultimately, this book is designed to accomplish two purposes: to allow students the room to write the things that are meaningful to them; and also to show them that their words have power to make a difference in the world around them—however small or large that difference may be. No act of courage, love, or caring is ever too small to count, and our hope is that this book may become a little act of love that creates some meaningful change.

Community-Forming Activities

(For English Classes, Wilderness Trips, Group Bonding, Role Development, Essentially: *Everything!*)

I. Trust Falls

The group breaks off into pairs (facilitator can choose pairs in order to ensure new partners). Each pair will practice trust. First, one person places hands across chest in an "X" fashion, then makes body straight and locks knees and back. Second person stands behind in "spotting" position: knees bent, arms extended, ready to break the fall of first person. First person says, "Ready, spotter?" Spotter replies, "Ready, _____ (name)." Falling person says, "Falling, spotter." Spotter says, "Fall away." This activity should be done three times with each person; as a pair becomes more comfortable, they can try closed eyes, farther falls, etc. But safety should come first! Facilitators should be aware of who is falling and when.

II. Elves, Wizards, Giants

This is a fun game to get groups active and involved. The group is split into two teams. Both groups are shown the signs for Elves (squat down and cup ears), Wizards (stand straight with arms out in front as if to cast spell), and Giants (stand tall with arms up high). A line is made down the middle of the field/court. Each group has a few minutes to gather at opposite ends of the field (their halves) and come up with a first-choice sign and second-choice sign. The facilitator calls both teams back to the center line. The teams line up, and the facilitator counts, "1, 2, 3 . . . GO!" As GO is yelled, both teams perform signs. Elves beat Giants, Wizards beat elves, and Giants beat Wizards. Whichever teams wins must chase the other team and try to touch them. All members that are touched now switch alliances. If members make it back to their home (the part of the field where they discuss signs), then they are safe. The process is repeated. If the same signs are shown, then teams revert to second-choice signs.

III. Get over the Barrier

A line of yarn or rope, or a meter stick, is placed a little above waist height (3–4 feet, higher or lower depending on level of challenge). Working as a whole, the group must try to get itself over the barrier without touching it. The group must be holding hands in a chain throughout the entire process, except for one break (one place where two hands do not have to be held). Once on the other side of the barrier, a member can let go of the hands. But he or she can only spot (standing close by with hands outstretched, to prevent any potentially injurious tumbles), not help lift others.

IV. Trust Walk

Students are blindfolded with handkerchiefs. The facilitator places students' hands inside those of other students. No talking can be made a rule to heighten the experience/challenge. The facilitator takes his or her place at the front of the line and leads students under trees, over obstacles, etc. (This can be made more or less challenging as the level of the group is assessed.) Afterward, a good discussion should ensue.

V. Make a Box

The group is blindfolded and placed inside a rope that is in the form of a circle. Group members must always have at least one hand touching the rope and must stay inside it. The objective is to make a box. For the first few minutes, they can talk; depending on how the group is doing (and whether the instructor wants the activity to be more or less challenging), the permission to talk may then be revoked. After an allotted time, the group then removes blindfolds to see how close they have come to making a box.

Debriefing/Discussing

Just as important as the experience of these activities is the debriefing that happens afterward. A mentor used to tell me, "You had the experience but missed the meaning." Debriefing helps to ensure that students will take home the meaning of what they've done, not just the fun or difficulty of the experience. Here are some good debriefing questions:

1. When did you feel most challenged? Why?
2. At what point in the activity did you have the most fun?
3. Name something that you saw someone else doing that you admired or thought was kind.

4. Did you see anyone challenge themselves or do something they thought they could not do?
5. If you could do it over again, what would you do differently knowing what you know now?
6. How do you think you did as a team?
7. Do the goals of the team and the goals of each person always line up? Why or why not?
8. What can we do as a team to communicate better and work more effectively together?
9. What are your personal strengths?
10. What are your personal weaknesses?
11. What are your strengths and weaknesses as a team?

At least some of these debriefing questions should be explored after each activity for about 15 minutes. Have fun, push forward, and remember what Eleanor Roosevelt said: "You must do the things you think you cannot do."

References

Adler, M. (1998). *The Paideia proposal: An educational manifesto*. New York: Touchstone.

Armstrong, K. (2006). What I wish I had known about marriage. *Glamour*. Retrieved from http://www.glamour.com/weddings/2006/07/kristin-armstrong

Avery, M. E. (2004). What is good for children is good for mankind: The role of imagination in discovery. *Science, 306*, 570–575.

Bitton-Jackson, L. (1999). *I have lived a thousand years*. New York: Simon Pulse.

Booth, W. (1988). *The company we keep: An ethics of fiction*. Berkeley: University of California Press.

Brown, D. (Producer), & Reiner, R. (Director). (1992). *A few good men* [Videotape]. Los Angeles: Columbia Pictures.

Buechner, F. (1993). *Wishful thinking: A theological ABC*. San Francisco: Harper. (Original work published 1973)

Burke, J. (2009). Reimagining English: The seven personae of the future. *English Journal, 99*(2), 12–15.

Collins, B. (2002). *Sailing alone around the room: New and selected poems*. New York: Random House.

Cranton, P. (Ed.). (2006). *Authenticity in teaching*. San Francisco: Jossey-Bass,

Dirkx, J. (2006). Authenticity and imagination. In P. Cranton (Ed.), *Authenticity in teaching* (pp. 27–40). San Francisco: Jossey-Bass.

Dostoevsky, F. (2004). *The brothers Karamazov*. New York: Barnes & Noble Books. (Original work published 1880)

Dufresne, J. (2004). *The lie that tells a truth*. New York: Norton.

Elbow, P. (1973). *Writing without teachers*. New York: Oxford University Press.

Ellis, D. (2004). *The breadwinner*. Toronto: Groundwood Books/Douglas & McIntyre Ltd.

Faulkner, W. (1950). *Nobel prize acceptance speech*. Retrieved from http://nobelprize.org/nobel_prizes/literature/laureates/1949/faulkner-speech.html

Fitzgerald, F. S. (2001). *The great Gatsby*. New York: Scribner. (Original work published 1925)

Flake, S. G. (1998). *The skin I'm in*. New York: Jump at the Sun/Hyperion Paperbacks for Children.

Freire, P. (1970). *Pedagogy of the oppressed*. New York: Continuum.

Hall, G. S. (1905). *Adolescence: Its psychology and its relations to physiology, anthropology, sociology, sex, crime, religion, and education*. New York: D. Appleton and Company.

Hansberry, L. (2004). *A raisin in the sun*. New York: Vintage Reprint. (Original work published 1959)

Hurston, Z. N. (2001). *Their eyes were watching God*. New York: Harper Perennial. (Original work published 1937)

Ingersoll, R., & Smith, T. (2004). Do teacher induction and mentoring matter? *NASSP Bulletin, 88*(638), 28–40.

Intrator, S., & Kunzman, R. (2006). Starting with the soul. *Educational Leadership, 63*(6), 38–42.

Jhally, S. (Producer and Director). (1999). *Tough guise* [Videotape]. Northampton, MA: Media Education Foundation.

Lamott, A. (1995). *Bird by bird: Some instructions on writing and life*. New York: Anchor Books.

Lester, J. (2000). Re-imagining the possibilities. *The Horn Book Magazine, 76*(3). 283–289.

McInerney, J. (1984). *Bright lights, big city*. New York: Vintage.

National Educational Association. (1894). *Report of the committee of ten on secondary school studies with the reports of the conferences arranged by the committee*. New York: American Book Company.

Palmer, P. (1998). *The courage to teach: Exploring the inner landscape of a teacher's life*. San Francisco: Jossey-Bass.

Ravitch, D. (2000). *Left back: A century of battles over school reform*. New York: Touchstone.

Reynolds, L. (2005, September 24). Keeping students excited about reading. *The Hartford Courant*, p. B1.

Reynolds, L. (Ed.). (2007). *Inside out and outside in: Essays on the nature and experience of love*. Moraga, CA: Stonegarden.net Publishing.

Rich, A. (1986). *Blood, bread and poetry: Selected prose 1979–1985*. New York: Norton.

Shirley, D., & MacDonald, L. (2009). *The mindful teacher*. New York: Teachers College Press.

Song, S. (2005, February 7). The power of make-believe. *Time*. Retrieved from http://www.time.com/time/magazine/article/0,9171,1025173,00.html

Twain, M. (2008). *The adventures of Huckleberry Finn*. New York: Barnes & Noble Classics. (Original work published 1885)

Wiesel, E. (2006). *Night*. New York: Hill and Wang. (Original work published 1960)

Woodward, K. (2004). Calculating compassion. In L. Berlant (Ed.), *Compassion: The culture and politics of an emotion* (pp. 59–86). New York: Routledge.

Yeats, W. B. (2000). *The collected poems of W. B. Yeats*. New York: Wordsworth Editions. (Original work published 1893)

Index

About the Author

Luke Reynolds has taught 7th- through 12th-grade English in public schools in Connecticut and Massachusetts as well as composition at Northern Arizona University. He is the co-editor of *Burned In: Fueling the Fire to Teach* (Teachers College Press, 2011) and *Dedicated to the People of Darfur: Writings on Fear, Risk, and Hope* (Rutgers University Press, 2009). Additionally, he is the author of *Keep Calm and Query On: Notes on Writing (and Living) with Hope* (Divertir Publishing, 2012) and *A New Man: Reclaiming Authentic Masculinity from a Culture of Pornography* (Stonegarden Publishing, 2007), and his writing has appeared in *Tucson Weekly, The Arizona Daily Sun, The Sonora Review, The Hartford Courant, Mutuality,* and *The Writer.* He holds a BA from Gordon College, an MA in Creative Writing from Northern Arizona University, and has done graduate work at Boston College's Lynch School of Education.